IGNITE

SETTING YOUR ORGANIZATION'S CULTURE ON FIRE WITH INNOVATION

LIBRARY OF CONGRESS CATALOGING-IN-PUBLICATION DATA

Moss, Randal C.
IGNITE: Setting your organization's culture on fire with innovation
by Moss, Randal C. and Neff, David J. p. cm.
Includes index.
ISBN 978-1-940858-17-3 (cloth); ISBN 978-1-940858-18-0 (ebk)

1. Innovation. 2. Business Transformation. 3. Business Strategy. I. IGNITE: setting
your organization's culture on fire with innovation/
Library of Congress Control Number: 2016935818

PROUDLY PRINTED IN THE UNITED STATES OF AMERICA

SPECIAL SALES VICARA Books are available at a special discount for bulk purchases
for sales promotions and premiums, or for use in corporate training programs. Special
editions, including personalized covers, a custom foreword, corporate imprints and bonus
content are also available.

For more information, contact the authors directly.

ACKNOWLEDGEMENTS

DAVID J. NEFF

First I'd like to thank God for letting me finish another book. That said lots of intelligent and patient human beings were involved in the creation of this book. The first person I want to thank is my amazing, entrepreneurial wife, Chelle. Besides being the love of my life, and making me laugh every day, she let me steal dozens of Sunday afternoons for writing, interviews and debating the finer aspects of this book with my co-author. I'd also like to thank my Dad, Mom and sister, Katie, for all of their support and my love of writing and reading growing up. The next person is my always hard working co-author, Randal C. Moss. A research field guide of this magnitude definitely takes a team. And I couldn't think of anyone else I'd rather write with, and debate with, than Randal. My only ask is that he move to a city with real BBQ and tacos soon. I'd also like to thank our amazing circus ringmaster and spectacular editor, LuAnn Glowacz. I'm glad she could take time from touring with Slipknot and her frequent visits to Lake Wobegon to help us. She proved to be the perfect taskmaster and part time cajoler that we needed. I'd like to thank Marnie at Vicara Books for helping us cross the finish line. And a special thanks to Rohit Bhargava for recruiting us to his publishing group and all the advice he gave us along the way.

RANDAL C. MOSS

This book took an exceptional effort to write and it was only with the support and partnership of others that I was able to bring this to fruition. I am eternally grateful to my wife Alison, and my three daughters for the inspiration and love that made all of the late nights of writing possible. My pride in this book pales in comparison to my pride in your accomplishments. I am in debt to my parents who put so much emphasis on education and drove me to a lifetime of learning. This is a testament to the passion they instilled in me, a passion I strive to instill in my children so that they may outachieve me. I am extraordinarily lucky to have David J. Neff as a writing partner. We have collaborated on two books, numerous speaking events and over a decade of work. In each new project we dare each other to achieve more. Thank you for issuing the challenge once again. While authors often get all of the credit, there is much to be said about our amazing support team; LuAnn Glowacz of WordCove, Chuck Wright at Wright Brain Graphics, Adam Rasmus at What.It.Is Design, and Rohit & Marnie at Vicara Books. Thank you all for helping us turn our idea into a reality.

CONTENTS

INTRODUCTION

INTRODUCTION

Do you remember Milton, the iconic character from Mike Judge's 1999 film *Office Space*? Milton was a personification of his company's inability to deal with change, bureaucratic processes, and a micromanaging boss. In the film, he suffered countless indignities and, finally, burned down his company's building after his desk was moved into the basement. Every time we see a red stapler, we're reminded of Milton.

How often, while at work, do you feel utterly dejected? How many of your employees report to work feeling the same way? Many workplaces have their own version of "the basement" just like in *Office Space*. It is the perfect modern metaphor for the place where brilliant ideas get cast away, never to see the light of day.

Our second book serves as a guiding light for organizations ready to give their smart-yet-frustrated employees a way to be heard and recognized. This book is intended to serve as a beacon for those organizations to harness the wisdom of their employees in order to improve performance. IGNITE is written as an instructional tool on how to "start fires" within an organization in order to tap the unused potential in every single employee.

It's time to bring innovative ideas out of the basement. It's time to create a new structure that reflects a strong internal culture, one in which employees are praised and rewarded for their contributions. It's time that those ideas have a chance to come to life through a purposeful strategy built around people, processes, and technology.

It is time to IGNITE innovation in your organization.

This book will prepare and inspire you—the reader—to drive results by actively implementing an innovation framework. Look around and you'll see for-profit corporations and nonprofit organizations of all shapes and sizes attempt this concept with varying results. The business world is filled with idea storms, creativity challenges and hack-a-thons, springboard initiatives, and idea labs. These efforts are aimed toward the same goal: creating more value.

Some of these efforts succeed. Most fail. This book will help you glean value from these systems and initiatives, explaining how and why some succeed while others fail. It will bring innovation programs to life in a simple, understandable way. No "corporate speak," no double talk. Just actionable advice, relatable examples, and compelling stories leavened with a few ounces of humor.

In our first book, *The Future of Nonprofits: Thrive and Innovate in the Digital Age*,[1] we took a deep look at what the future of the nonprofit industry looked like. Neither we, nor our readers, came away liking the future we saw. Nonprofits were concentrating on the here and now and not thinking about the future. There was no long view, no attempts to future-proof from iterations and changes in the market. Moreover, we saw that attempts to engage stakeholders in collaboration were mismanaged and met with cynicism. Nonprofit corporate cultures were not primed for participatory innovation and, so, attempts by the few brave souls within the culture to ignite it fell flat.

---

1 Call us biased, but we really think you ought to read this book, too: David J. Neff and Randal C. Moss, *The Future of Nonprofits: Innovate and Thrive in the Digital Age* (New Jersey: Wiley, 2011). Find it on Amazon at http://www.amazon.com/The-Future-Nonprofits-Innovate-Digital/dp/0470913355.

Then we realized many for-profit organizations were making the same mistakes.

We walked away asking a few big questions of these organizations: Do you know that your core customers and a lot of your internal employees have solid, actionable ideas about what you could be doing better? Are you even listening to them? And, if you are, what are you going to do with the ideas and concepts that you do hear?

That was when we had an amazing realization: We could help future-proof both for-profit and nonprofit organizations by changing their cultures into those that actively listen to employees and pay heed to their new ideas. Various ancient cultures around the world believed that to truly change one's "being," one needed to be burned to the ground in a great fire. The proverbial Phoenix that rose out of this fire was a clear look at a person's true self. This book is all about moving organizations of all types (enterprise, large, small, local, nonprofit) to set fire to their static, boring, idea-destroying internal cultures. Unlike the company in *Office Space*, which literally burned to the ground because of the frustration of its employees, your company can potentially burn away the noise of its old ideas and systems and emerge with a new way of harnessing ideas and energy.

Every good fire starts with an ignition source. Today we hand you the match. IGNITE is more than just the name of our book, it is the name of our innovation framework. We want this to be the book that takes you from exploring ideation to executing it.

Thanks for letting us serve as your internal arsonists.

David J. Neff and Randal C. Moss

Chapter 1:
What Is Innovation?

In the beginning is an idea. Not innovation; not a world-changing product or ultra-premium service or a disruptive business model. Just an idea.

The path from idea to implementation is littered with the remains of incomplete concepts and failed ventures. It is a graveyard of forgotten dreams and unfinished business. Left in the ruts are fragments of potential brilliance. Along the culverts remain products and services that nobody needs or wants.

But it doesn't have to be this way.

Innovation can help a business develop by growing an idea into something tangible, but it's an exceptionally messy process. It can be nonlinear in nature and almost impossible to predict. But it doesn't need to be that hard, that convoluted, that unpredictable. That is what the IGNITE Framework is all about. It's about overcoming chaos and making sense of the innovation process so that you can maximize your investments and bring stability to what could otherwise be an impossible venture.

This book is not about what is or isn't innovation. However, it's important to understand the definition of innovation in order to harness its potential to create new products, services, programs, or even real world experiences.

Quite simply, innovation is something newly created or introduced. To qualify, though, it must be unique and new in a meaningful way. As we unmask the IGNITE Framework throughout this book, it is important to recognize that the process of innovation applies to all classes of outputs.

No matter what a car manufacturer tells you, that fifth cup holder in an armrest is not innovation. Nor is innovation a schema of consolidated debt obligations with credit default swaps to insure certain losses. And it's likely not another luxury spa treatment for pets. Innovation is a new way to create real, measurable value.

A Brief History Lesson

One of the first academics to write about innovation was Joseph Schumpeter, an Austrian economist who was born in 1883. Schumpeter is credited with being the first thinker to bring the study of innovation into the academic realm. He set forth three critical components to moving value forward in a business cycle: invention-innovation-diffusion.[1] Through his research and publications, Schumpeter argued that inventions became innovations only when they were put into use and delivered value.

Notice that we said "delivered value," not "delivered the value that was originally intended to be delivered." This is an extremely critical distinction. Innovation—even within the confines of a regimented process like the IGNITE Framework—can discover previously unforeseen value. It is up to us to recognize it when it happens and to decide whether or not to capture it.

---

1 Darius Mahdjoubi, *"Schumpeterian Economics and the Trilogy of 'Invention-Innovation-Diffusion,'"* last revision: January 24, 1999, https://www.ischool.utexas.edu/~darius/17-Schumpeter-innovation.pdf.

For examples of this point, you need look no further than some of today's most popular and groundbreaking prescription drugs for men. Propecia— now commonly used to treat male pattern baldness—was originally Proscar, used to treat benign enlargement of the prostate. Viagra—well known as the grandfather of all penile dysfunction medications—was originally used as a treatment for symptoms of heart disease.[2]

The general goal of innovation is to drive measurable progress through change, to create incremental value, and to improve processes, products, and experiences. It's important to view innovation with this wide lens and resist the urge to focus on tangible products. Economists and academics are adept at this. The IGNITE Framework is designed to help business leaders reach this sweet spot, in order to better enable the process of moving an idea from the point of inception through a process that transforms it into innovation.

In developed economies, mature businesses need to find ways to continuously grow their revenues. Innovating new products and categories are key tactics of their growth plans. However, improving the efficiency of the innovation process is now more critical than ever before. The Procter & Gamble Company (now commonly known as P&G), one of the world's leading consumer packaged goods companies, continuously innovates new products. P&G's cross-functional innovation process is responsible for products such as Swiffer® and Febreze®. More importantly, though, the process is responsible for innovating the product categories of dry dusting and odor elimination.

P&G's Executive Chairman of the Board (and former President and Chief Executive Officer) A.G. Laffley places an emphasis on strategic growth through new innovation and product development. According to Laffley, a high-functioning innovation process is critical to the success of P&G's business units and the enterprise as a whole. The company spends

2 Haley Sweetland Edwards, "6 Hugely Successful Products Invented for Something Else," mental_floss, January 26, 2012, http://mentalfloss.com/article/29840/6-hugely-successful-products-originally-invented-something-else.

nearly $2 billion annually on R&D. That's roughly 50 percent more than its closest competitor.[3]

As with all process developments, there needs to be a level of investment to put a proper framework into place. And invest you will. The brutal fact is that there is no free solution that can serve as an innovation engine, creating long-term idea development at your organization. It takes staff resources, budget, time, and technology costs to maintain a forward-thinking and forward-moving innovation center and to develop a culture that supports it. In the long run, however, our research and experiences strongly support the assertion that this investment is worth it.

We both first experienced the power of a well-run innovation program while working together at the American Cancer Society. Since that time, we've seen the value of these types of innovation programs show themselves in the real world. Throughout this book, we'll be writing more in length about the American Cancer Society's Futuring and Innovation Center and other innovation programs at Dell, Starbucks, AT&T, and dozens of other organizations. These well-known programs are implementing, in one way or another, facets of the five core components of the IGNITE Framework.

Introducing the IGNITE Framework

The IGNITE Framework is a process for the identification, development, and implementation of innovations. It provides order and structure to the process of innovation, while addressing the fundamental business requirements and concerns that arise in the real world. It is predicated on the reality that time and resources are scarce and, in some cases, more valuable than the outcomes of work effort, which means they must be protected, measured, and managed with great care.

3 Bruce Brown and Scott Anthony, "How P&G Tripled Its Innovation Success Rate," *Harvard Business Review*, June 2011, https://hbr.org/2011/06/how-pg-tripled-its-innovation-success-rate.

Like most frameworks, IGNITE provides a set of guidelines that enables leaders in any organization to establish a process that fits their needs. The framework is set up like a traditional stage-gate waterfall process, where ideas must pass through prescriptive stages and clear milestones before they can move on to the next stage. This is a key part of the development process. It protects valuable scarce resources and ensures that only the strongest and most viable concepts make it through to full funding.

IGNITE, also like most frameworks, is designed to be flexible and scalable to fit almost any organization's size. It allows a large organization the opportunity to scale to meet its capacity and gives a small organization the option to implement a powerful tool to efficiently advance its work.

As we progress through the book, we will address each of the five core components of the IGNITE Framework:

1. Organizing to IGNITE

2. Farming Ideas

3. Trial by a Jury of Your Peers

4. Business Plan Canvas and Value Articulation

5. Building and Launching a Proof of Concept

First, let's take a look at a brief overview highlighting key points in the process, along with the questions you'll want to ask yourself along the way. After all, as Albert Einstein has been credited with saying, "If I had an hour to solve a problem and my life depended on the answer, I would spend the first 55 minutes figuring out the proper question to ask."[4]

---

4 This particular quote from Albert Einstein has been referenced with slight variances for decades. We chose the version posted by David Gurteen, accessed December 1, 2015, http://www.gurteen.com/gurteen/gurteen.nsf/id/determining-the-proper-question.

As you collect ideas

We begin the IGNITE journey by collecting ideas. Seems simple enough, right? But the key to success in this step of the framework is in loading the top of the funnel with *quality ideas* that are *relevant* to your business and your business goals. Resist the temptation to stuff the idea collection mechanism full of concepts that are either not relevant to your organization's core skill set or will not create value (or value that is meaningful to your organization).

Part of an excellent collection process is setting the stage and making clear your expectations of what will be submitted. The challenge that this presents is that the number of ideas you collect is going to directly correlate to the size of the net that you cast. Providing an abundance of criteria for submissions will intrinsically shrink the number of ideas gathered; the inverse is also true.

If you ask for the world from your teams and employees, don't be surprised when it shows up on your doorstep.

When planning idea collection, you—as the innovation lead—should think about the following key questions. The answers you come up with will help you refine your collection criterion and inform your collection strategy. The questions you ask are just as important as where you ask them and of whom you ask them.

- Who will we ask for ideas?
- Should we only ask employees or should we widen the net?
- What kind of ideas will we collect?
- Is there a specific process or method of collecting ideas we should follow?
- Should we measure how effectively we promote our collection effort?

- When will we collect ideas?

- How will we inspire others to submit ideas?

- What should we offer as incentives as part of idea collection?

As you review ideas

Once collection is complete, it's time to move into a very formal and rigorous review process. In our own research and evaluation efforts, we've seen a pattern develop. Every company that we learned about (including our own) had a formal and rigorous idea review process in place. Not all review processes were the same…and that's OK. But, in every case, every idea was evaluated against a host of metrics before any resources were invested to move it forward.

A second commonality was that the review processes were built with one single purpose in mind: to filter out the ideas against a set of criteria including business alignment/mission, economic viability, and business capacity. Each organization asked a different set of questions, but they were all fundamentally rooted in checking the idea against the above principles.

Finally, in each process we've been a part of, the team undertaking the review of the ideas shared similar attributes. These review teams were relatively diverse in their constitution. They included participants with varying work functions, socio-economic backgrounds, genders, and ethnicities. Every organization has their own idea about who should be on the team (frankly, the team makeup is often a reflection of the company culture as a whole).

As you begin to move forward with your process and establish your review criteria and review team, these are some key questions to keep in mind. They will help guide you in your development but should also serve as challenge questions to keep you true to the mission of innovation development and out of the business-as-usual rut.

- What are the steps of our review process?

- Who will do the reviewing?

- Do we have an organizational skills bias to overcome?

- Does our organization have the right culture for our review process?

- What would we like the outcome of our review to be?

- What questions will we ask during a review session?

- What are the specific criteria that will determine if an idea is worth investing in?

- How will we know if an idea is the right fit?

- What will we do with great ideas that are not a great fit?

- What will we do with ideas that are a great fit but are not extraordinary?

As you refine ideas

The ideas that first come into review are going to be general and without much focus. Expect this and appreciate it. These ideas are going to come in from all across and, sometimes, if that's your goal, outside of the organization. Those preparing and submitting these ideas may not have the skill or experience to craft and submit a formal and well-developed business plan. An exceptional review process gives a review team the ability to see the value in each idea and what it could be if it were fully developed and implemented.

The idea refinement and business plan development process is critical not only for an idea's transformation but also for the idea submitter's transformation. Creating a formal business plan, for one, forces the idea submitter to take a more comprehensive ownership stake in their own idea's success. This step also helps to codify the core elements of the ideas, as well as clarify the costs and resources necessary to make the testing and learning come to life.

During the business plan development stage there are a number of questions you will want to address with the person who came up with the idea (or, as we refer to them throughout the book: the ideator). These questions will help lock in the finer details of the concept.

- Who will create the business plan and what template (or form) will they use?
- How will we sell this to our organization?
- What are the basic elements needed for a prototype?
- What is the responsibility of the launch team to help make it work?

As you consider funding

Funding innovation is risky business. But that's essentially what innovation is: a risky bet on a new and unproven idea. At its core, the IGNITE Framework is a risk management tool. It exists not only to ensure every idea that gets funded complements the business, but that each idea is a financially viable option for the business to undertake.

In our current business environment, we have choices on how we can invest our capital. And, as good stewards for our organizations, we're compelled to make choices about what investments will deliver the best return. Innovations present a fundamental challenge to this notion because they are untried and possibly perilous. With this in mind, we've looked at a few other organizations to see how they set up their funding for new projects and programs and have come up with some key questions every organization should be asking before earmarking innovation budgets.

- Where should the cash come from: retained earnings or debt?

- How will we justify the funding expenditure in the face of other options?

- What will be our appropriate level of funding needed to usher an innovation through the proof of concept phase?

- Who should manage the finances through the trial phase and beyond?

- Who within the organization should own the P&L of the prototypes and why?

- How have other organizations funded similar projects?

- What 'return calculation' will we use in our funding decisions? (Be consistent with your organization if they use Net Present Value, Internal Rate of Return, or Modified IRR.)

As you run the proof of concept

Without question, one of the most exciting and nerve-racking steps in the IGNITE Framework is developing and executing a proof of concept (POC), which is the prototype, or model, of the proposed innovation. We often think of the POC as a lighthouse. This built prototype, or lighthouse, serves to illuminate the dark spaces around your idea, and show others where it's safe to tread. IGNITE is not just an intellectual exercise in developing ideas that look good on paper; it is about taking those ideas and getting them to market quickly. The POC phase is critical because it is the data collected here that will determine if the innovation moves on to the next stage of the process.

Part of the challenge of this POC phase is making sure that it is designed correctly. It must deliver the data you need to make an informed "go-forward" decision. Quite simply, the POC should answer the question, "Does this thing really do what we think it does?"

To design a POC worthy of answering that question, you'll need to answer these questions first:

- Who will run the trial?

- Who will support the trial?

- How long should the trial last?

- How much should it cost (funding)?

- What will we do with the prototype before the trial and after it (set it up for success)?

- How will we overcome organizational jealousy, politics, and other barriers?

- How will we celebrate success and learn from defeat?

As you launch

One of the most famous innovation projects in U.S. history is the Lockheed Martin Skunk Works® program founded and run by Clarence "Kelly" L. Johnson. In 1943, the project launched to deliver the United States Air Force its first jet fighter. To accomplish this, the Skunk Works team was handed a nearly impossible timeline, yet completed their project one week early. What allowed Johnson to operate Skunk Works so effectively and efficiently was his unconventional organizational approach. He broke the rules, challenging the current bureaucratic system that stifled innovation and hindered progress.[5]

Critical to their success was the culture of innovation that Johnson infused into his team of engineers and the 14 managerial principles to which they adhered (principles we'll discuss further along in this book). The idea

---

5 For more on Lockheed Martin's Skunk Works® program, see: "Skunk Works® Origin Story," accessed September 8, 2015, http://www.lockheedmartin.com/us/aeronautics/skunkworks/origin.html.

of Skunk Works was an innovation in and of itself: an organization within an organization that was protected, funded, and allowed to truly manifest its own destiny. That concrete structure, independence, freedom to take risks, and rewards for success are important themes we will highlight throughout the book.

When it comes to planning your own launch, set yourself up for success by answering these questions:

- How will we properly evaluate and sell an innovation for full production?
- Who within the organization will own it post-trial?
- Who will get credit for the monetization revenue?
- How will we leverage success to attract more interest in the process and then repeat it all over again?

This Is All About Change

The whole premise of innovation, the reason we are passionate about it, is that change is seated deep in our genes. We know, deep down inside us, we have a choice to make. The old adage is true: We can evolve or we can die. In life, as in business, we constantly face that decision.

"It is change, continuing change, inevitable change, that is the dominant factor in society today. No sensible decision can be made any longer without taking into account not only the world as it is, but the world as it will be."

We featured this quote by renowned science fiction author Isaac Asimov in our first book, *The Future of Nonprofits: Innovate and Thrive in the Digital Age*,[6]

---

6 David J. Neff and Randal C. Moss, *The Future of Nonprofits: Innovate and Thrive in the Digital Age* (New Jersey: Wiley, 2011).

but it speaks so well to the IGNITE Framework today, we resurrected it here. It was Asimov's observation that society is in a perpetual state of change, ever evolving and growing in complexity. Change is inevitable to your organization as well. The only difference from organization to organization is in how well the energy of change is harnessed.

When we finally accept the wisdom of Greek Philosopher Heraclitus of Ephesos, who gifted us with the knowledge that the only constant is change,[7] we begin to consider the value in managing change for our own benefit. The IGNITE Framework is custom-built to generate the tools requisite for managing perpetual change.

With each interview we conducted for this book, we came closer to understanding how the employees we spoke with are working through a constantly evolving scenario. Once they have their odds and ends sorted out, the rules of the game change. The only difference between them and, perhaps, you, is that they've learned to move beyond and ahead of rule changes, leapfrogging the changes that will certainly come naturally, and becoming change-makers themselves.

Some call this disruption. Others call it first-mover advantage.

We call it purposeful innovation and recognize the unlimited value it holds for the organization that can embrace, master, and implement it. The IGNITE Framework is the blueprint for this very type of innovation factory. It's only waiting for a leader who is ready to become the change.

---

7 *"Heraclitus of Ephesos,"* Ancient History Encyclopedia, accessed September 8, 2015, http://www.ancient.eu/Heraclitus_of_Ephesos/.

Chapter 2:
What's Wrong With Your Internal Culture?

Before you implement the IGNITE Framework, you will need to take a close look at your organization's internal culture. It may be a shaky foundation that needs some renovation. Or it may be ready to truly accept the change. Think about your own experiences: How many jobs have you left or job interviews have you walked away from because the culture didn't fit your personal belief system?

To say an organization's culture can lead to problems is an understatement. Diane Vaughn wrote in her book *The Challenger Launch Decision* of the absolute failure of culture at NASA in the 1980s; one that may have ultimately contributed to the Space Shuttle Challenger explosion. A series of communications failures resulted in the drifting apart of communication channels that existed between NASA subcultures. These channels included an engineering subculture, which had warned the rest of the organization that the O-rings used to seal certain joints in the space shuttle would fail in cold weather. It was a warning that, Vaughn said, fell upon deaf ears due to managerial neglect and other cultural breakdowns. [1]

It's likely (and fortunate) that cultural weaknesses within your own organization probably won't lead to disaster on such an epic scale. However, Vaughn presents a striking example of how your organization's culture can affect communications and trust.

For example, if your culture is too rigid, it won't accept risk. Organizations that cannot accept risk cannot fail forward or handle experimentation: qualities needed for an innovation system to work.

In what is considered one of the most influential management books of all time, *Organizational Culture and Leadership*,[2] Edgar H. Schein defines culture as a powerful, tacit, and often unconscious set of forces that determine our individual and collective behaviors, ways of perceiving, thought patterns, and values. That's a lot to take in, we know. Let's break that down into a simple way to evaluate the current culture at your company.

How to Evaluate Your Organization's Culture

Schein identified three levels of culture present in any organization. These are:

1. Artifacts: Visible organizational structures and process (which can still be hard to decipher).

2. Espoused beliefs and values: Strategies, goals, philosophies (and even justifications).

3. Underlying assumptions: Unconscious, taken-for-granted beliefs, perceptions, thoughts, and feelings (the ultimate source of values and action).

---

1 Diane Vaughn, *The Challenger Launch Decision: Risky Technology, Culture, and Deviance at NASA* (Chicago: University of Chicago Press, 1997).

2 Edgar H. Schein, *Organizational Culture and Leadership*, 4th Ed. (San Francisco: Jossey-Bass, 2010).

If this concept seems highly abstract, it is. But take half a day (during existing time, meetings, etc.) to assess your culture through artifacts, espoused values, and underlying assumptions. Suddenly, what was abstract will become more concrete. Once all is revealed, you'll better understand your own organization's cultural breakdowns and how they might stand in the way of igniting innovation.

Start with the level of artifacts. What do you see and hear when you walk around your workplace? What's the dress code? Does your staff recycle or compost? Do people bus their own dishes into the sink? What artwork is in the hall? These are all the artifacts of your cultural workplace. It's easy to observe and even "feel" some elements of culture at this level.

At this point, you are probably wondering why these norms exist or how they were formed. You'll want to get to the bottom of who made these decisions in the first place. But don't. That comes later. Instead, take 10 minutes to write down every visible artifact you see around your workplace on a sheet of paper or into a digital notebook like Evernote.

The next level is espoused values. Now it's time to ask the questions you started to uncover when you looked around for artifacts. What's the real justification behind the dress code, open desk policy, all the closed doors for managers, etc.? Some of the answers can be found in the employee handbook. You know, that old binder collecting dust on your shelf? At a chemical company for which our co-author David consulted, all new employees were given a book called "Working Right" that espoused company values and a commitment from the executive leadership team to back up these values. The same book went on to explain why these values were formed and gave concrete examples of people who lived these values, day in and day out. It was a physical manifestation of what values the company lives by every day.

The consulting agency where David once worked hung the following sign on the wall in the entrance. It's a great way to remind employees what the company stands for.

In addition, every employee received two booklets when they joined the company: One explained company values and the other explained consulting competencies. As an example, the value of "Curiosity" is explained here:

Definition	+ Signals	− Signals	Correlating Competencies
Being eager to learn more about people, tools, and technology helps us grow.	Asking exploratory questions	Indifference	Creative Insight
	Proactively research and discovery of insights for our clients and business	Resisting change	Customer Commitment & Foresight
	Trying new things and approaches	Exerting minimum effort	Strategic Insight & Prioritization

While your own organization may not have such extensive documentation, take 10 minutes to re-read whatever it is your organization provides to make its values clear to your staff. Maybe they're simply posted up on the wall when you walk in, or hidden away in a break room. Maybe they're posted on your organization's website. Once you've found them and read them, or talked to someone who knows them, ask yourself: Do I notice any inconsistencies? For instance, are freedom of thought and flexibility espoused as values, yet you run as a "command-and-control" kind of business? Is one of your stated values "curiosity," yet no one's ever asked for questions at the end of a staff meeting or stood up to ask a question at a town hall event? Or, when you have town hall events, does your leadership not even bother to introduce themselves? Pay attention to what is not lining up and write it down.

The last level is underlying assumptions. At this point, you'll be reaching deep inside your company culture. According to Schein (again, in his book *Organizational Culture and Leadership*), the essence of culture can be found when jointly learned values and beliefs work so well, they are taken for granted. That can be both good and bad. For instance, think about your organization's history. Where and when did it start? Did it have a single founder? Multiple co-founders? Was it purchased by another firm and the founders were displaced or forced to retire? Or did they earn out when it was purchased and quickly leave? Was it founded by hippies in the 1960's looking for a new way for nonprofits to save animals, or MBA students out of the University of Texas looking to disrupt an existing technology field? These underlying emotions, values, and historical facts are all legacies of the people who founded your business. They have far-reaching, complicated effects on the way your business works today.

Take 10 minutes to consider the underlying assumptions about working where you work, based on the questions above. Armed with such extensive legacy knowledge, you'll find yourself seeing the commonalities between what the organization "stood for" and what it represents presently. That's OK, for now, because it feeds into the next step.

Now, take 10 more minutes to informally talk to the newest person in your office (an intern would work well). Ask them what they think are the top five unmentioned elements of your culture that they uniformly obey. You'll be surprised at the difference in the two lists.

Snapshot of a Broken Culture

Leaders of any organization have a tremendous responsibility to change, keep, or impose culture on employees and staff. After completing the half-day evaluation outlined above, you should have a clear picture of the state of your organization's culture.

Not happy with what you see?

In order to change it, you should understand the reality of what constitutes an organizational culture. When it comes to organizational culture specifically, Schein has viewed it as a "pattern of basic assumptions which are invented, discovered, or developed by a given group as it learns to cope with its external adaptation and internal integration. These basic assumptions must have worked well enough to be considered valid and, therefore, to be taught to new members of staff. [Organizational] culture is the right way to perceive, think, and feel in relation to problems."[3]

With that in mind, let's look at how to change culture by changing the assumptions we transmit.

Leadership has a lot to do with setting the cultural tone. What the leaders of an organization decide to measure and pay attention to, how they react to crisis, and how they allocate resources are all ways in which they transmit what should be of value and importance in their organizations.

---

[3] Co-author Randal found this specific quote in his own 1st ed. copy of *Schein's Organizational Culture and Leadership* (San Francisco: Jossey-Bass, 2004).

Furthermore, the criteria they use to recruit, the role modeling and coaching they provide to their subordinates, and even the criteria they use to give rewards sends cultural information into the organization. Schein groups all of these activities into 'Primary Embedding Mechanisms.'

He goes on to discuss 'Secondary Mechanisms,' which focus more on physical space and construct as well as the practices and mythology that give the organization its identity. He states that the hierarchical structure of departments, processes and procedures, and even the physical layout of the buildings all have strong bearings on culture. Where people sit—in relation to each other, the hierarchy, and the reporting tree—impacts employee perception. These physical constructs accompany the typical rites and rituals, myths and legends, and even the formal value statements impacting the way employees see their organization at a peer level.

So, how do you begin to repair this culture? How do you shift your culture to support and embrace innovation? Taking into consideration all of the factors above, a cultural shift is a slow and measured effort that begins at both the leadership and grassroots levels. It involves changing the habits of leadership to support innovation, promote innovative thinkers, and reward those making headway and achieving success. It involves changing the myth narratives to focus on these great innovators and the outcomes of their efforts. And it involves updating formal value statements.

A broken culture is not ready to enact change through innovation. But don't be discouraged. We firmly believe that one single idea can change an organization. And we also firmly believe that one person can work to change an organization's culture as well. It just may not be able to happen the way you might assume.

Take the following scenario, for instance:

A new CEO was brought in to head up a small beverage company in Austin, Texas. The challenges for someone in her position are grand. The beverage industry in the U.S. is constantly shifting through mergers and acquisitions. It's subject to increasing legislation and government actions around advertising to minors and adults, advertising in schools, calorie counts, and more. She also knew that the space contained hundreds of competitors from companies that make everything from bottled water to energy drinks, including giant soft drink companies with billions of dollars of revenue, all fighting for shrinking shelf space in retail stores and the shrinking attention spans of modern consumers.

With all of this in mind, her first order of business was to rectify a lack of innovation in the company. She launched an ideation platform very similar to what we recommend within the IGNITE Framework.

But it failed. At every turn.

A group of consultants were brought in to dissect the situation. They found a fundamental problem with the culture. In previous years, this beverage company had modeled itself on a very tightly structured system of finding the best solution, documenting the hell of out of it, placing it in tightly controlled folders on a state-of-the-art enterprise collaboration system, and rewarding employees for using the solutions in those documents. If that was not how you liked to work, they were happy to show you the door. Previous CEOs and managers had encouraged this system, and it worked. They had become a successful beverage business in a tough market throughout the early 2000s.

But now, the new CEO realized, something was wrong. This tightly controlled environment was at odds with what she knew had to happen. The company needed to free itself from putting only one solution forward, hiding it away on the network and rewarding people for following the rules. It needed to innovate or die.

She promoted idea submissions through the employee newsletter, encouraged ideation in her all-hands meetings and added suggestion boxes in the hallways. But employees were ambivalent. If she had stopped to really observe the culture, she would have looked at a different solution. As counterintuitive to the innovation process as it may seem, she would have had more success going along with the culture, at least at first. Perhaps she could have made innovation a part of the rules, as something that was measured (as it should be). She could have encouraged employees to meet innovation goals set forth in their annual performance plans. She could have done this while hiring people with innovation as a part of their profiles. Over time, she could have changed the culture into one that ignites innovation.

Does this sound like your organization? Are you ready to start changing your organization for the better? What does a good culture of innovation actually look like?

Lockheed Martin's Cure for Culture Clash

For an answer to that last question, we can look to a culture that was developed not in 2015, but in 1943. Lockheed Martin is an American global aerospace, defense, security, and advanced technology company that is one of the world's largest defense contractors. Sounds like it would be a pretty rigid culture, right? Wrong. Lockheed is one of the oldest vanguards for innovative company culture. And it all started in 1943, when the U.S. government approached Lockheed about building a new fighter jet.[4] The fighter jet was to be named the XP-80 and the project was to be top secret. As we briefly mentioned in the previous chapter, a young engineer named Clarence "Kelly" L. Johnson was picked to lead the team that would build the plane in complete secrecy, away from the rest of the organization.

Now, to get into more detail than we did in the last chapter, we have two interesting points to dissect. Why would Lockheed pick a young engineer

---

4 More of the Skunk Works origin story can be found here, accessed September 9, 2015: http://www. lockheedmartin.com/us/aeronautics/skunkworks/origin.html.

to lead such a big project? And why did they need to develop the project outside the usual organizational constraints?

Lockheed recognized they needed a new, fresh approach to this project. And Johnson fit that bill (we'll get to that reasoning in a minute). They also needed the project to be a secret so it wouldn't be subjected to the normal, painful, bureaucratic process. Instead, this innovative project could have a license to operate outside of the normal system—something necessary in order for it to be accomplished quickly. And it certainly was accomplished quickly, in record time. In fact, the team designed and built the XP-80 in only 143 days: seven days ahead of schedule. Can you imagine how excited the U.S. Department of Defense must have been? Meanwhile, much of the business world can't even get a social media marketing campaign out on time, much less a week early.

This process was so successful that it spawned its own division within Lockheed called Skunk Works®.[5]

So what was the process behind this idea-turned-reality in 143 days? Although often credited to Johnson, this process formed over many years of work by the Skunk Works team and continues to evolve at Lockheed today. Let's take a look at a few of the core tenets of the Skunk Works process—lovingly called "Kelly's 14 Rules & Practices"[6]—and how they could work in your organization.

Rule 1: The Skunk Works manager must be delegated practically complete control of his program in all aspects. He should report to a division president or higher.

While a modern innovation process needs checks and balances to make it successful, we do agree that authority and autonomy are very important.

5 Do you ever wonder how Skunk Works got its name? The story includes the "Li'l Abner" comic strip and a strong brew made from skunks and old shoes. Read about it here, accessed September 9, 2015: http://www.lockheedmartin.com/us/aeronautics/skunkworks/origin.html.
6 *"Kelly's 14 Rules & Practices,"* accessed September 9, 2015, are still followed at Lockheed today. They can be found at: http://www.lockheedmartin.com/us/aeronautics/skunkworks/14rules.html.

In fact, they are hallmarks of the IGNITE process. The group you select to lead your innovation efforts needs authority to choose the best ideas and fund them. And those who hatch these great ideas need the ability to execute on their ideas, independent from their other work responsibilities.

Rule 2: Strong but small project offices must be provided both by the military and industry.

The lesson here? Give your innovators the support they need to execute on their idea. This support does not need to be grand in scale (nor should it be, in order for the team to stay agile). And, these days, the support team does not even need to be tied together geographically. Can you devote project management support from Atlanta even though the developers are in Austin? It can still work.

Rule 3: The number of people having any connection with the project must be restricted in an almost vicious manner. Use a small number of good people (10 to 25 percent compared to the so-called normal systems).

Project teams dedicated to innovation must be small and able to practice agile pivots as needed around the program, process, or product. Later on in this book, we'll give you an idea of the exact combination of personalities you may want to select for this small-but-mighty team.

Rules 5 and 6: There must be a minimum number of reports required, but important work must be recorded thoroughly. There must be a monthly cost review covering not only what has been spent and committed but also projected costs to the conclusion of the program.

We're lumping these two points together to highlight how important reporting and budget considerations are in any quality innovation process. No leader or innovation team should be allowed to go "lone wolf" on a project.

Rule 9: The contractor must be delegated the authority to test his final product in flight. He can and must test it in the initial stages. If he doesn't, he rapidly loses his competency to design other vehicles.

We've skipped further ahead to this important point. The team must not only build a prototype of the product, process, or program but they must also be in charge of testing it through a proof of concept or a 'lighthouse.' A lighthouse is much like a pilot program that is built on rocky ground, battle-tested, and, if it succeeds, helps others within the organization find their way to success. You may not feel your organization is able to undertake such an endeavor with employees right now. That opinion may change by the end of this book. (By the way, Lockheed sure uses "he" as their pronoun here a lot, don't they? Please forgive their 1943 stereotypes while we keep moving along.)

Rule 11: Funding a program must be timely so that the contractor doesn't have to keep running to the bank to support government projects.

That's a simple but bold statement. When designing and creating an IGNITE Framework at your organization, be sure to allocate funds to cover such things as development costs, staff, process building, dev/coding (if needed), and the building of the proof of concept. Too often, teams building a product come up against a brick wall built by the lack of funds to test in the market.

Rule 13: Access by outsiders to the project and its personnel must be strictly controlled by appropriate security measures.

Yes! Sequester everyone on the team until the work is done! Kidding, of course. Outside of national security matters, the IGNITE Framework encourages the opposite: open and honest collaboration between teams building your product, process, or program and the existing structure of your organization. "Show and tell" or "demo days" are an integral part of getting the buy-in of the larger organization at all points of development. As simple as it sounds, the folks at Google in New York have casual "Beer & Demo" events every Friday. Most of you will not need a military level of secrecy around your projects. In fact, for most of us, running secret programs can inadvertently cause paranoia and gossip within the organization that can do more harm than good.

Rule 14: Because only a few people will be used in engineering and most other areas, ways must be provided to reward good performance by pay, not based on the number of personnel supervised.

Hopefully, at your organization, employees are measured in more modern ways than the number of personnel they supervise. Instead, they can be measured on business objective outcomes and, for more specific employees such as fundraisers or sales people, they can be measured on specific number-based goals. What about an innovation team? Did they achieve their goals? Did they launch their program, project, or product? Did they stay in budget and regularly report and share their progress? Were they able to do this AND maintain their objectives with their normal jobs? We'll get into specific success measures for your IGNITE system later in this book.

Innovation in a Family-Run Business Culture

Another unique area in which innovation often meets with major resistance within the company culture—and, particularly, the leadership—is within family-run businesses. We're not necessarily talking "mom and pop" shops, here. Family-owned firms like BMW and Walmart account for a combined $6.5 trillion in annual sales, enough to be the third-largest economy in the world.[7]

In its latest survey of U.S. family-owned businesses, the accounting and consulting giant PwC found that over one-third of current family-business leaders worry that an innovative leadership style isn't necessarily baked into the family's DNA. On the contrary, their hunch is that having family members in key positions at the company can make the firm less open to new thinking and ideas. More than 65 percent view the need to continually innovate as a major challenge.

However, PwC calls out family-run businesses that have found ways to overcome these innovation obstacles by embracing the fresh thinking that can come when new generations take the helm. J. Miles Reiter, CEO, Driscoll Strawberry Associates, Inc. reveals one such idea—born out of a refreshed culture of innovation—that he thinks may have saved the company from suffering the "third generation" curse that so many family-run businesses face. Among other changes, Reiter oversaw the development of Driscoll's innovative clamshell containers—the clear plastic boxes, holding strawberries, which are now a common sight in groceries everywhere. This innovation, in fact, is likely sitting in your fridge or on your kitchen counter right now.

"I would say that as much as half our growth would not exist without the clamshell," he explains. "The mesh baskets we had been using before were overwrapped, took a lot of labor, and got crushed in your shopping

---

7 Chase Peterson-Withorn, "New Report Reveals The 500 Largest Family-Owned Companies In The World," *Forbes.com*, April 20, 2015, http://www.forbes.com/sites/chasewithorn/2015/04/20/new-report-reveals-the-500-largest-family-owned-companies-in-the-world/.

cart. They were also hard for the retailer to handle, whereas the clamshell packages are easy. And because we can put our name on the packaging, we've really seen significant growth in brand awareness."

As Reiter boldly adds, "I think every generation has had a period of going broke, a sort of reinvention."[8] Innovation, as evidenced here, has the potential to deliver value in organizations large and small, public, private, and even family-owned.

Creating an Upstart-Worthy Culture of Innovation

We sat down with Ben McConnell, author of the books *Citizen Marketers: When People Are the Message*[9] and *Creating Customer Evangelists: How Loyal Customers Become a Volunteer Salesforce*.[10] McConnell had this to say about the differences in internal company culture between upstart companies and established companies:

- Upstart companies focus on creating markets. Established companies focus on defending markets.

- Upstart companies love simplicity because it produces faster results. Established companies are mired in complexity because it creates job security.

- Upstart companies know that innovation is like test-riding a new roller coaster. Established companies come up with 100 reasons why amusement parks are dangerous.[11]

---

8 PwC's seventh family business survey and the Driscoll innovation story can be found at: "*Professionalize to optimize: US family firms are no longer winging it*," PricewaterhouseCoopers LLP, last accessed December 1, 2015, http://www.pwc.com/us/en/private-company-services/family-business.html.
9 Jackie Huba and Ben McConnell, *Citizen Marketers: When People Are the Message*. (Chicago: Kaplan Publishing, 2007).
10 Jackie Huba and Ben McConnell, *Creating Customer Evangelists: How Loyal Customers become a Volunteer Salesforce*. (Lewis Lane Press, revised edition 2012).
11 These comments and more throughout the book by Ben McConnell are from a series of written interviews with the authors in 2014 and 2015.

So where is your organization on that front? Don't worry if that's a hard question to answer or if the answer is, "Get us off this roller coaster right now!" Even one person pushing hard against a wayward culture can start to make a difference. Now, no miracle worker can completely change the culture alone. But, even at corporate mammoths we might not think of as being innovative, one person can plant the seed of change.

To illustrate this point, we asked Michael A. Foster, now a senior product manager at EBay, Inc., about his work on innovation at Microsoft. In particular, we asked Foster about Microsoft's history with (or without) open innovation, a specific business practice in which an organization uses both internal as well as external ideation.[12] Here's what he had to say:

> **IGNITE Authors:** Did Microsoft embrace the idea of open innovation early on?

> **Foster:** Open innovation typically involves getting ideas from outside the organization. The open source model is the best known of these. As you may have guessed, Microsoft was not a leader in this area in the mid-2000s. We attempted to change that culture, but had limitations from the top on implementing such concepts. Our focus instead was on grassroots innovation.

> **IGNITE Authors:** So, then, how did Microsoft's internal innovation program start?

> **Foster:** A general manager named Jon Pincus was the catalyst for this. He was founder and CTO of a company that Microsoft

---

12 The concept of open innovation was explored by University of California Adjunct Professor Henry Chesbrough. You can read more about it in Chesbrough's book, *Open Innovation: The new imperative for creating and profiting from technology*. (Boston: Harvard Business School Press, 2003).

acquired. He wore bright pink pants, psychedelic shirts, and had full-on Einstein hair, so he stood out at the Microsoft campus. I immediately connected with him. He was very good at securing funding and had a simple, straightforward (if not challenging) mission: *To change the culture of Microsoft.* That is, from a purely top-down culture in which senior executives decided what the priorities and products would be, enforced by a (strict) review process to a culture where grassroots innovation—bottom up, from any level in the company—could thrive.[13]

IGNITE Authors: How did it work?

Foster: Well, it was pretty grassroots! There wasn't a playbook in the mid-2000s for innovation programs in large enterprises, so we did many different things and saw what worked. We had seminars for ideators—people with ideas—and offered to coach them on how to pitch their ideas and get traction for them. We, of course, did the all-night hackathons (we called them Mashup Days) and had prizes and recognition for the winners, like showing your prototype to Bill Gates in person.

IGNITE Authors: How were you funding it?

Foster: Jon was very good at securing funding. When most Microsoft budgets start with "B's" [Billions], the fact that Jon's budget for these seminars and events annually cost less than an "M" [Million] pretty much went as noticed as a fly on the wall by the money counters. But it got plenty of notice by the employees.

---

13 We can tell Pincus is an interesting guy. Just check out his LinkedIn photo: https://www.linkedin.com/in/jdp23.

Building this process from the ground up at a place like Microsoft was no easy task. In an environment where patents—and the profits they bring in—reign supreme, Foster admits it was a hard road at times.

> **Foster:** Presenting an idea to an executive or a patent attorney is a challenge no matter the quality of the idea. Executives are short, sometimes bullying, and at best, tell the 'I've heard this idea before' story before hearing the full idea. I've found prototypes, mock-ups, and visuals—even a quick video—to be far more effective than the usual words plus PowerPoint pitch. I encourage everyone to build a prototype, even if it's a paper one. You'll get further with images than words. A mock-up is worth a thousand slides. [14]

Remember Ben McConnell and his comparison of upstart versus established company culture? He also revealed to us his simple, yet brilliant theory on how important follow-through is to the culture of any organization, no matter how young or old it may be.

"The theory is simple: Company culture is the non-stop display of company values," McConnell said. "When a company's actions consistently correspond to its language, culture is successful. In other words...you are who you say you are. When actions don't correspond to language, dissonance sets in. Then [comes] mistrust, which breeds hypocrisy. Finally, there's outright contempt. By that point, the culture is a mess. Turnover becomes an expensive problem, and brand reputation suffers. The marriage is over."

McConnell is no stranger to either type of environment. As a vice president of the startup business consultancy Ant's Eye View (where he worked alongside IGNITE co-author David), he helped shape the organization's core practices and strategic direction. When we asked

---

14 These and subsequent insights from Michael A. Foster are from an email interview with the authors, February 21, 2015.

McConnell about the specific culture that made Ant's Eye View such a success, he highlighted a couple of key points.

"Company founders tend to hire people they like, and who are like them," he explained. "Therefore, company culture is often a direct reflection of two things: the founder's values and personality traits. In the early days, we spent a lot of time talking about what we didn't like about our previous companies' cultures and the elements that caused dread when the alarm clock went off. It's a good exercise: We don't like this, this, or this."

If you take one thing away from this chapter, let it be what McConnell said next:

"[We sat down and] we defined the enemy of good culture."

Simple yet powerful. Before you sit down to implement the IGNITE Framework or any other innovation platform, ask yourself if you have a forward-thinking culture that fosters innovation. Your answer may define your biggest obstacle to success. If your culture is not ready for this kind of innovative thinking, you may have some work to do before you begin to engage your intrapreneurs.

PEOPLE POWER

Chapter 3:
Who Are Entrepreneurs
and Why Hire Them?

"I have not failed. I've just found 10,000 ways that won't work."

—Thomas Edison[1]

In this book, we will talk in depth about innovation, the innovation process, and the corporate culture necessary to support internal innovation initiatives. We take time in this chapter to really focus on the individuals who drive innovation forward from the inside out: the ideator, the program manager, the innovator, or—as we like to call them—the intrapreneur.

Thomas Alva Edison is arguably one of the most prolific inventors of all time. Over the course of his life, he filed and accumulated 1,093 U.S. patents, as well as many patents in the United Kingdom, France, and Germany. You may recall learning in grade school that Edison was

---

1 This and other Thomas Edison quotes can be found here, accessed September 11, 2015: http://en.wikiquote. org/wiki/Thomas_Edison.

the "Wizard of Menlo Park, New Jersey" and that he was responsible for inventions like the motion picture camera, the light bulb, and the electrical grid. But you probably never learned about his amazing entrepreneurial skills.

According to the *The Cyclopædia of American Biography*, Edison started one of his first businesses—*The Grand Trunk Herald* newspaper, which he typeset, printed, and sold with four assistants—while only in his teens.[2] Edison was a serial entrepreneur with the innate ability to invent his own products. He possessed a business savvy second only to his amazing prowess in the art of invention. (Some, like *The Oatmeal* creator Matthew Inman, would even argue that his business savvy outweighed his penchant for invention and that his contemporaries like Nikola Tesla were the true scientific geniuses. But that doesn't necessarily negate our next point.)[3]

It was Edison's business savvy that kept the lights on (literally) in his famous laboratories. But he didn't stop there. He was able to take a single invention (the light bulb) and use it as the foundation for what is today one of the world's largest companies (General Electric Company). He was able to then take the invention of the electrical grid and use it as a basis for Edison Electric Company. Consolidated Edison, Inc., Edison's little electric company, has since become one of the largest investor-owned energy companies in the U.S., with approximately $12 billion in annual revenues and $40 billion in assets.[4]

Electricity was the foundational element upon which Edison built an empire. With it, he both created and fulfilled needs. Lighting up the night, riding home via street cars, X-raying broken bones, heating coffee, and ironing shirts were just some of the ways in which Edison's inventions transformed American life. Edison's ability to invent was epic, but his ability to take invention and build business around it was what truly

---

2 James E. Homans, "Edison, Thomas Alva," The Cyclopædia of American Biography. (New York: The Press Association Compilers, Inc., 1918.)

3 Tesla was awesome but, perhaps, he could have benefitted from some of Edison's business savvy. See The Oatmeal's take here, accessed September 11, 2015: http://theoatmeal.com/comics/tesla.

4 According to GE's 2013 Annual Report, accessed September 11, 2015, http://www.ge.com/ar2013/pdf/GE_AR13.pdf.

elevated him above his peers. In every sense, he was an entrepreneur working to see his dreams come true. Edison was motivated by the desire to see his inventions become part of everyday life. In today's parlance, we would call this a quest for commercialization. And commercialize is what Edison did very, very well.

From his laboratory in Menlo Park and his winter home in Fort Myers, Florida, Edison and his team diligently worked, developing new inventions and then creating markets from them. One of Edison's young engineers took the principles of entrepreneurship very seriously. Though he was 20 years younger than Edison, he played an integral part in the lab's success. In return, the culture of the lab had a lasting impact on this young apprentice. That young man was Henry Ford, founder of the Ford Motor Company.[5]

Beyond all the patents, accolade, inventions, and companies, what made Edison's lab so special was the culture of experimentation and support that it nurtured. It drove the engineers and tinkerers within to aspire to achieve great things. The environment around Edison was teeming with brilliant thinkers and skilled chemists and engineers. On their own, these individuals would have produced some interesting things. But reaching the level of proficiency and prolific production needed to make an impact required resources and support. How long would it have taken, and at what cost, for these inventions to have come about on their own? Success would have certainly been less likely.

This culture of innovation has been replicated throughout the decades, hitting its stride now with large nonprofits like Greenpeace, as well as technology giants like Google and Apple. It's a culture that's difficult to replicate in many organizations and is something that Walter Isaacson tackles in his biography of Steve Jobs, since Apple has had to change its approach to innovation over time (as has Greenpeace and Google). The natural transition from outgoing CEO Jobs to incoming CEO Tim Cook

---

5 Learn more about Edison and Henry Ford's history together here, accessed September 11, 2015: https://media.ford.com/content/fordmedia/fna/us/en/features/ford-s-legacy-of-sustainability.html .

is a period of time worthy of dissection. As Haydn Shaughnessy of *Forbes* reports, while Jobs believed that there were a handful of Apple employees who could really drive innovation and innovative thinking at the company, Cook believes that the DNA of all employees who work at Apple should have innovation at its core. According to Cook, "Innovation takes place at the intersection of hardware, software and services."

Critics may say that companies like Apple and Google—and even Edison's General Electric—risk losing their innovative edge the larger they become. The truth is this: Large or small, for-profit or nonprofit, an organization that invests in intrapreneurs—and gives them what they need to innovate—will benefit from them.

More and more, larger organizations are figuring this out. Shaughnessy suggests "the rules of innovation are changing...the ideas around disruptive and sustaining innovation, which put executives on the edge of their seats in fear of smaller rising stars, are losing their relevance."[6]

Instead, large companies are expanding their portfolios of products to enable innovation. Google X labs, for instance, has launched everything from driverless cars to Google Glass, high-altitude Wi-Fi balloons, and glucose-monitoring contact lenses.[7] With Google's continuing evolution, Apple has had to stay competitive and harness maximum creativity from its employees. (We'll talk more about both companies' innovation programs later in the book.)

Look at the underlying efforts of both Google and Apple and you'll find a concentrated and intentional move to empower employees and execute calculated risk taking. It's a culture of entrepreneurialism within the confines of the corporation, far beyond and more aggressive than the typical and traditional project development efforts in most companies. And

6 Haydn Shaughnessy, "Tim Cook's New Innovation Strategy For Apple, Right On Time," *Forbes*, July 2, 2013, http://www.forbes.com/sites/haydnshaughnessy/2013/07/02/tim-cooks-new-innovation-strategy-for-apple-right-on-time/.
7 Jon Gertner, "The Truth About Google X: An Exclusive Look Behind The Secretive Lab's Closed Doors," *Fast Company*, April 15, 2014, http://www.fastcompany.com/3028156/united-states-of-innovation/the-google-x-factor.

let's be honest: Neither Google nor Apple is a typical, traditional company. Their atypical growth results make that statement loud and clear. We believe that one of the factors of that growth is a direct result of their investment in employee intrapreneurs.

This is the value of the intrapreneur. But let's take a second to define that term. An intrapreneur is an individual who can, within the walls of an existing business, bring forth an idea/concept/invention and dedicate his or her time to turning that whim into a new product or business line extension. It is this intrapreneur that is the critical component to your internal growth engine. However, having these unique personalities on your payroll does not necessarily guarantee you success. It's what you do with your brilliant intrapreneurs that will dictate the success of your company or organization.

These employees have something in their DNA. Call it an entrepreneurial streak or maybe an eye for solving problems and answering the questions others can't. They can work independently but, more importantly, they can work seamlessly as part of an integrated team at your organization.

Are you creating a culture in which they can thrive? Do you even know where to find intrapreneurs? Do you have any idea how to recruit them and interview them? Let's find out.

First Things First: Look in the Mirror

Before you begin your search for intrapreneurs both from within and outside your organization, take a genuine look at yourself and your corporate culture. As we investigated in the previous chapter, your organization's corporate culture likely discourages intrapreneurs from doing what they do best. However, you may not fully realize this within your own organization— even as you have followed our advice in this book thus far. Why? The way an organization handles new ideas and the way its employees and stakeholders view how it handles new ideas may be incongruent. Unfortunately, in this case, perception is reality.

Take time to reflect and consider the situation facing your organization. Be honest with yourself because the way your employees and stakeholders perceive your operation is more important (at this point) than how idea development within your organization is actually set up.

So how are you handling things? Take this quick quiz. Feel free to circle or highlight more than one answer (it's OK, you can write in the book!).

A. Our employees think that we foul up every new idea we touch, and they're pretty much correct.

B. Our employees think that everything we touch turns into gold but, in reality, it is bronze, at best.

C. Our employees think that we foul up every new idea we touch but, in reality, we have a good track record of launching profitable products.

D. Our employees think that everything we touch turns into gold, even though we're surrounded by the still flaming, but about-to be-burnt-out carcasses of failed launch attempts.

Considering the scenarios above, you'll realize we are boiling down this issue to substance versus perception. This next section is dedicated to helping you address the perception part because addressing perception is the first step in igniting your existing intrapreneurs. If you cannot credibly show that you are making strides toward implementing a meaningful innovation program, you will never convince the hidden intrapreneur within your organization to step up and participate. Instead they will sit back, bide their time, and wait for another suitor to come along who will make the most of their talents. And, these days, that wait isn't long.

Fixing Your Perception Problem

It may be easier than you think and may cost a lot less than you could ever imagine to fix your perception problem. In organizations we have worked with, we have seen that there are certain ways to present idea development efforts that garner genuine interest from the employee base. The key, as we see it, is to be:

1. Transparent and celebratory in your successes.

2. Publicly introspective in your failures.

3. Welcoming in your outreach.

4. Reasonably transparent in your process.

While these four elements may seem contradictory, they work well in concert to maintain interest and drive excitement among employees and stakeholders.

Transparent and celebratory in your successes

All too often, companies call mass meetings, press conferences, and investor calls to launch new programs and new products with no mention about who was responsible for the success. We accept the impossibility of naming every single designer, engineer, or product manager who touched a product or program during development. But why do we accept that reality? From books and movies, we have learned that giving credit where credit is due is part of our culture. Even video games have credits that roll at the end of the game. However, this route leads to the movie credit effect: a slew of names that flashes by too quickly to read, let alone comprehend.

However, there must be some level of transparency when it comes to recognition. Re-watch former Apple CEO Steve Job's monumental iPhone product launches announcement from 2007.[8] You may notice Jobs brings

---

8 If you missed Steve Job's iPhone product launch announcement in 2007 (or simply want to relive it), watch it here, accessed December 3, 2015: http://www.youtube.com/watch?v=t4OEsI0Sc_s.

onstage executives from Cingular, Yahoo!, and Google, but makes no mention of his own team. He does not acknowledge that there were hundreds and potentially thousands of brilliant minds who put effort into making the iPhone a reality. Is it conceivable that the iPhone just happened? No? So why not give credit where credit is due? If you've read Walter Isaacson's biography of Jobs,[9] you'd have some idea on why this happened. It's food for thought, nonetheless.

Publicly delivering praise has a positive and uplifting effect on both those who have contributed to an effort and to the company as a whole. By being publicly transparent about the individuals who contributed to a milestone, you are showing that, as an organization, you truly value the individual effort, even if it is the employee's everyday job to be great.

Consider this kind of public praise a reinvestment into the innovation effort. When employees and outside stakeholders see that contributing to ideation can earn them praise, and that the company genuinely appreciates their contribution, they will be more inclined to participate.

Publicly introspective in your failures

We all want our products and programs to be successful and to deliver above and beyond projections. No one likes to admit defeat. The reality, however, is that defeat is inevitable. What's more, defeat and failure can be helpful. So why is it that organizations always try to sweep failures under the rug instead of using them as a lesson learned? Take Apple, for example. Do you remember their failures? What about the underwhelming Apple LISA, Newton, and the TAM?[10]

Failures present an opportunity to be open and honest. In the examples mentioned above, Apple most likely learned that design had to be accompanied by powerful and functional computing technology.

9 Walter Isaacson, *Steve Jobs* (New York: Simon & Schuster, 2011).
10 For these and other Apple flops, see: Bryan Gardiner, "Learning from Failure: Apple's Most Notorious Flops," *Wired*, February 24, 2008, http://www.wired.com/2008/02/gallery-apple-flops/.

Hiding failures, especially failed innovation projects, only discourages the teams who worked so hard on them. Sweeping failures under the rug and sanitizing the past sends a message that the organization was not invested in the project and is not interested in learning from the hard work that went into development.

The reality is that the postmortem of a failed project can be just as valuable as a go-forward plan for a successful innovation. Publicly owning failures while showcasing lessons learned gives your organization the chance to reward risk takers instead of placing blame. It gives the organization as a whole insight into issues they should be aware of as they think of new ideas.

As we mentioned at the beginning of this chapter, Edison is known to have once said, "I have not failed. I've just found 10,000 ways that won't work."

Welcoming in your outreach

Every success is an opportunity to invite more people to participate in the innovation effort. A successful project or product launch celebration is the perfect time to make a call for new ideas and additional participation. Taking the time to offer praise and appreciation to both the innovation team and to the individual innovator shows those within the organization and its stakeholders how valuable their contributions are.

This brings to mind a personal moment which perfectly illustrates this point. While working together at the American Cancer Society in 2005, we collaborated on the mobile cancer information tool (for the Palm Pilot) that would later be known as C-Tools.[11] David was the creator and project innovator and Randal was working as the leader of the Futuring and Innovation Center (FIC), the sponsoring entity. The project had gone through the full FIC development cycle and had shown tangible value to the organization.

---

11 For more on American Cancer Society's C-Tools, visit its Wiki page, accessed December 4, 2015: http://psychology.wikia.com/wiki/C-Tools_2.0.

At that time, the American Cancer Society had just over 3,000 nationwide employees and had a practice of holding bi-annual update meetings in which the then-CEO, Dr. John Seffrin, would present the state of the organization and announce new strategic initiatives and plans. It was during the spring semi-annual business update in 2005, just after the product went live in February, that Dr. Seffrin asked Mike Mitchell, national vice president of the FIC, to address the national audience and speak about the success of C-Tools.

The presentation was not just about the success of the C-Tools program, but about the success of the FIC. On the coattails of that success, Mike asked everyone in the organization to engage and participate. He asked for *every* idea—big or small, simple or complex. He made the innovation process approachable and fun. And, most of all, he set a welcoming and inclusive tone for coming years.

That following week, FIC received more idea submissions than it had gathered in the prior two years of operation. More than 150 ideas came in for consideration. Regardless of the value those 150 ideas delivered, the fact is that being inclusive, welcoming, and asking for contributions makes every stakeholder feel important and helps deliver results.

Relatively transparent in your process

This element is best explained through a story. A story about a prolific chef named Jeff Conley, who is so adept at his craft he can concoct the most amazing meals on a whim out of practically nothing. Below, Randal describes a particularly great conversation with his friend, Chef Conley.

"When Chef Conley would visit me and my family, he would cook up a storm in our modest kitchen. But there were always two rules: He never let us into the kitchen when he was cooking and he always cleaned up his mess when he was done. During a visit one summer, we had a conversation about these two rules.

The conversation came up only after the rest of the family had gone to bed and the bourbon started flowing. After plenty of cajoling, he finally explained these rules.

'Some things in life are messy by nature. They just are. No matter what you do, you are going to create a big damn mess making it happen,' Chef Conley told me. 'Cooking is one of those things. I don't care how careful you are, how slow you go, you are going to make a big damn mess. So you might as well just accept that as a fact and move right along with your life.

'But see, here is the problem: Nobody wants to look at a huge mess right before they eat a gorgeous meal. Great food has to be as visually appetizing as it is delicious. You eat with your eyes, too! Nothing turns my appetite off more than a sink of dirty dishes, sloppy counters, and a filthy apron.

'Think about it. If I served the rib roast tonight in a blood-spattered apron with a burnt-out roasting pan and stained butcher block as a backdrop you would have thought to yourself, 'Eww. So that's where dinner came from.' There goes the appetite right out the window. Nobody wants to see that, man. Especially when I want them to be paying attention to my standing rib roast. I worked hard on it and I want your attention here, on your plate, not thinking about the mess you have to clean up after dinner.

'Think about the open kitchen concept in a restaurant. You get to see those guys grilling the chops and fillets live and in person. You get to see your food being made so you appreciate it a bit more, and it is believable. But you still don't see all of the dirty dishes, and messy prep-work that goes on in the prep kitchen behind the wall. That would just kill your appetite.

'At the same time, you have to believe that what I am doing has some value. You have to see that I did not sit you down in your living room and run out the back door and do a fancy-up number on some carry-out food, or heat and dress up a frozen dinner. So I intentionally left out the mixing bowl with the glaze. And I leave out some minced herbs — in case you want more — but also to let you know that

this is a real meal. That, yeah, I did it myself, and that it took me a lot of effort to do it. You see that real work went into this meal and therefore you appreciate it that much more."[12]

This is the basis for relative transparency, the idea that you want everyone to see and appreciate the hard work going into the innovation process, but want to conceal the unappetizing components that may turn them off. It's important to be purposeful and genuine in what you share. The politics, the trial and error, the success and failure can all leave behind a lot of mess that may cloud the end product. Working with intrapreneurs can be challenging. If you have any hope of keeping your new innovation pipeline moving, you will put some concerted effort into Chef Conley's concept. Clean up most of the mess and leave out enough to show that, indeed, hard work happened here.

The processes and mechanics of innovation development, which we will get into in coming chapters, are best left to those participating in the development of those innovations. By no means are we preaching that the innovation process should be overly exclusive or secretive. There is a balance between creating allure around a magical process and creating an unapproachable process that feels off limits to outsiders. The IGNITE Framework can help keep that balance in check.

The Intrapreneur's DNA

So what makes the intrapreneur tick? One of the most difficult challenges you will encounter as you begin to work with intrapreneurs is their unique motivations and drivers. These motivations and drivers are not only unique to the rest of the workforce and stakeholders but are rather individually unique as well. At their core, intrapreneurs share a desire to steer their own ships and control a portion of their destinies, but they have

---

12 Based on a conversation between co-author Randal and Chef Jeff Conley, Summer 2008, in Cincinnati, Ohio.

varying reasons for wanting the opportunity to do so. Being able to predict and placate those underlying desires will help you draw in, engage, and retain intrapreneurs with great success.

Like Edison, intrapreneurs tend to be creative, curious self-starters who have a knack for problem solving and take pride in pushing the boundaries of what is possible. Unlike their very close relative the entrepreneur, intrapreneurs thrive within the framework of an organization. To an extent, they show a penchant for calculated risks (albeit with other people's money) and have the self-starting drive to make good on the bets they place.

Unsatisfied with the status quo, intrapreneurs are often looking for the next thing to do and next project to work on. They seek out new experiences within their organizations because they are often looking for an edge that will help them better develop and launch their ideas internally. Their passion for cross-training is a clear giveaway. Gaining experience and exposure to various areas of the organization and developing a network of connections is a hallmark intrapreneur move. They are simply positioning themselves to launch their next big idea, whenever it may bubble up to the surface.

Not necessarily overt overachievers, intrapreneurs have an uncanny ability to harness energy and focus when they are working on a passion project. They often work extra hours, take on extra work in group meetings, and display greater leadership — as long as it contributes to the development of their innovations. Classic intrapreneurs never let their self-created additional workload get in the way of their everyday job responsibilities.

Finally, we've noticed intrapreneurs tend to be social and thrive on idea exchange. They are predisposed to be curious and are constantly on the hunt for another interesting project. To an intrapreneur, the monotony of the daily grind is tolerable. They are not entrepreneurs for a reason and get a certain level of satisfaction out of the consistency a corporate environment provides. A corporate social environment is good for the intrapreneur because it provides them contact with many other people, perspectives, and ideas.

By now, you're beginning to understand how to recognize innovative employees, the value they bring, and the importance of how they perceive your innovation environment. The bottom line is that intrapreneurs have so much more to give to your organization than your organization may be truly equipped to foster. Let's break down this issue further by looking at the "substance" part of substance versus perception. What can you offer that will find and keep innovative employees, and keep those employees innovative?

Our co-author David's own experience at the American Cancer Society mirrored this path. After attending several conferences in 2006, David had an idea for developing a mobile tool for primary care physicians to help diagnose signs of cancer. After collecting his ideas and writing a basic outline, he went to his boss at the time, Vice President of Communication Danny Ingram. During this time, David was leading the charge on website, intranet, and online community development, with online fundraising being a major part of his job. (As you can see, mobile software development and product management was not in that job title.)

Ingram then suggested he submit the idea to the Futuring and Innovation Center. Once David's idea was accepted into the center, he followed a process similar to the IGNITE Framework we describe in this book. It would have been a lot easier for David's boss to say no to the idea. For him to say, "Why don't you get back to work on the website and that fundraising database?" You have to realize that this was nearly a decade ago and the idea of mobile anything was something brand new. Would physicians use these types of tools while in the room with patients? Who would beta test this tool? Should a nonprofit get into the software business at all? (As a side note, it's interesting that most large organizations that David and Randal consult for are still having that conversation today.)

David developed the software (later called C-Tools as we mentioned before) for PDAs, not mobile phones. That's right, personal digital assistants. At the time, the software was actually created for black and white (or was it green?) Palm Pilots. Remember those? Again, David was the director of online communications, not the director of mobile or software development. Yet, it was an area he was passionate about. The American Cancer Society saw that and let him pursue it within the walls of what was a predecessor to the IGNITE Framework.

And it succeeded. It was a victory for the organization—there were thousands of downloads all across Texas—and for David as an intrapreneur. Managing a team of software developers, marketers, and customer support experts was something that David realized he was good at. Since that time, David has led and organized many other software developments and has successfully launched apps for Best Friends Animal Society and, more recently, a mobile CRM called FyleStyle for iOS in 2015.

How to Spot an Intrapreneur

So, again, you ask, "How do we find these people?" *Harvard Business Review* contributors Vijay Govindarajan and Jatin Desai have some ideas.[13]

"Intrapreneurs can transform an organization more quickly and effectively than others because they are self-motivated freethinkers, masters at navigating around bureaucratic and political inertia," they wrote.

Govindarajan and Desai go on to outline ways in which to recognize an intrapreneur. Essentially, intrapreneurs are people who:

- Feel money is not the measurement: The ability to influence is more motivating than reward.

- Are obsessed with strategic scanning: Intrapreneurs are always looking at what's next.

---

13 Pinchot University Blog, "What is Intrapreneurship?," accessed December 4, 2015, http://pinchot.edu/what-is-intrapreneurship/.

- Believe in greenhousing: Ideas are contemplated internally as they develop.

- Thrive on visual thinking: Brainstorming, mind mapping, and design thinking are important.

- Are good at pivoting: Intrapreneurs can make significant shifts from current direction.

- Value authenticity and integrity: Intrapreneurs strike a balance between confidence and humility.

Keep these traits in mind as we take you through some real-world applications.

Seek "wanderers"

Remember that David attended several conferences before his idea took shape at the American Cancer Society. In an upcoming chapter, you'll see the top conferences we recommend for intrapreneurs and their management. One of these is SXSW. The annual Austin gathering brings together not only the best minds in the technology world, but the film and music worlds as well. With the addition of SXSW ECO, EDU, and V2V, that now includes the best minds in education, sustainability, and entrepreneurship. This cross-pollination is what makes the conference the best place to see what's happening...two years from now.

The employees who beg to attend conferences like SXSW are what Govindarajan and Desai call strategic scanners. This is a good thing. You want employees who don't dread attending conferences. Instead, you want them actively bugging you for learning and development funds so that they can attend. Not every employee is a thought leader (someone who not only wants to attend, but wants to speak on behalf of your brand) and that's OK. If you have one of those people sitting in front of you in a job interview, we suggest you award extra points.

Here's what to ask: While interviewing, ask job candidates about the last three conferences they attended. What were their favorite speakers or panels? Why? You're not looking to be sure they did their homework. You're looking for passion, for an intense interest in soaking up as much knowledge as they can.

Test visual thinking

While David interviewed for his position at Ant's Eye View, he was asked about his most recent book on nonprofit digital strategy. Instead of just talking about the book, he jumped up, grabbed a marker, and drew a simple diagram on the board to help illustrate the book's purpose. This simple act was something that impressed his future boss, Ben McConnell.

There's great power in "getting your butt out of the chair" and walking up to the whiteboard during an interview. It's not so much as having design skills or the ability to draw, or even portraying a sense of bravado. Instead, it's about the ability to think visually. To take an idea and map it out, and to do it spontaneously in front of colleagues or friends (or strangers), is a vulnerable move.

What to ask: Ask job candidates to "map out" an idea they turned into a reality at their last job. Someone with intrapreneurial tendencies will naturally look around for a pen or marker or will find some other way to show, not just tell.

Look for an ability to pivot

"So you tried it this way and it didn't work? What did you do then?" you ask the job candidate. The candidate replies, "Well, I just moved on."

That's not the answer you want to hear. That's not the tenacity you need from an intrapreneur.

Although the term 'pivot' has undergone major overuse by every entrepreneur on the TV show *"Shark Tank,"* we want you to not be afraid to use it in your hiring conversations. Why? It's a simple, understandable idea: Concept A was attempted. They tested it. It didn't work. The candidate pivoted to a new approach or application and tested it.

As Jay Samit says in his book *Disrupt Yourself,* "Pivoting is not the end of the disruption process, but the beginning of the next leg of your journey."[14]

What to ask: If the idea of pivoting doesn't come up when a candidate describes previous work, this could be a red flag. Even so, here's a test situation that colleagues of ours use. Ask the candidate to play out the following scenario:

> *You are a struggling business owner whose business is not doing well and whose rent is becoming a severe liability on the business. You have an investor who comes in and promises $150,000 in investment for a different space to help you grow. Part of the term sheet is that you have to break your current lease. What strategy would you use to break the lease?*

Acceptable answers may be to consult a lawyer about the contract or to find a real estate agent that can help locate a sub-leaser. Plenty of different answers work. What you're looking for are those that prove the candidate is a quick problem solver.

Why Take the Risk?

The fact is, 70 percent of entrepreneurs say they left previous corporate roles because they felt too confined.[15] However, when done right, intrapreneurship is beneficial to organizations and workers alike, even if those workers seem to be free-spirited entrepreneurs. Providing a structured environment that involves the right people, processes and open innovation can actually help valuable ideators

---

14 Jay Samit re-released this book in July 2015 as *Disrupt You! Master Personal Transformation, Seize Opportunity, and Thrive in the Era of Endless Innovation* (New York: Flatiron Books, 2015).
15 Mai Thi Thanh Thai and Ekaterina Turkina, *Entrepreneurship in the Informal Economy: Models, Approaches and Prospects for Economic Development* (New York: Routledge, 2013).

stay happy within your organization. The myth is that ideators use the resources of a bigger organization to come up with new ideas and then, when it works, they leave to start their own company.

Storyhackers Co-founder Ritika Puri explains, "These leaders look great on paper but can have trouble adapting to larger organizations. First and foremost, entrepreneurs are difficult to retain because they'll likely want to start another company. Second, there's a perception that entrepreneurs aren't trustworthy—that they're more likely to spend more time chasing their own business ideas than furthering their employers' objectives."[16]

Thus, as Puri goes on to point out, there's a real debate going on in the hiring world about the value of approaching and hiring entrepreneurs into an existing system. The other side of the argument is that investing in innovative people is necessary if an organization wants to grow or stay competitive in today's marketplace.

David Armano, vice president at Edelman Public Relations, explains that "in a world filled with fast-moving change, a large organization that becomes complacent and loses sight of the benefits of having an entrepreneurial streak built into their massive global systems can find themselves disrupted in short order."[17]

In short, hiring entrepreneurs can be worth the risk. Would you rather have three employees walk out at the same time to start a new business or have three employees who never advance, never have new ideas, and never challenge the status quo? Within your organization, are there roles that require risk taking? Roles that require you to solve for ambiguity? Roles in which process needs to be brought forward? These are perfect roles for the entrepreneur-turned-intrapreneur. Just be sure the job candidate has the desire to work within the structure of an organization, as we outlined previously.

---

16 Ritika Puri, "4 Things Recruiters Should Know About Hiring Entrepreneurs," *LinkedIn Talent Blog*, September 23, 2014, http://talent.linkedin.com/blog/index.php/2014/09/4-things-recruiters-should-know-about-hiring-entrepreneurs.

17 David Armano, "Move Over Entrepreneurs, Here Come The Intrapreneurs," *Forbes*, May 21, 2012, http://www.forbes.com/sites/onmarketing/2012/05/21/move-over-entrepreneurs-here-come-the-intrapreneurs/.

How to Retain an Intrapreneur

Now that we've taken some of the fear and mysticism out of hiring ideators, let's spend a few minutes investigating ways to "feed and care for" this endangered species, which requires some evolutionary thinking.

Let's first take a look at the company inome (yes, that company name is lowercase), which is now named Intelius, and was founded by Naveen Jain. After researching prize-based crowdsourcing (which we'll discuss later in the book), Jain saw that incentivized prizes have been successful motivators throughout history, reaching as far back as the Longitude Act of 1714 and the Orteig Prize of 1919.[18]

Spurred on by this newfound inspiration, Jain designed the inome iPrize Challenge to generate ideas for the company while giving the internal ideators a chance to pocket some cash. One such idea was submitted by employee Elisabeth DeVos, who imagined a gaming application built on the premise that everyone has "six degrees" of separation from everyone else. The concept is to allow users to look up a name and then determine the connections they share using different search paths. This type of evolutionary innovation helps keep intrapreneurs engaged while they help develop inside your organization. The extra cash doesn't hurt, either.

In 2009, John Donovan, now senior executive vice president of AT&T Technology and Operations, launched AT&T's The Innovation Pipeline (TIP), which acts as sort of stock exchange for employee ideas. Employees can submit and vote on ideas using TIP's online "crowdsourcing" platform available 24/7. Ideas are refined through real-time feedback from peers, with the best rising to the top through a star ratings method.

Funded ideas are then quickly developed into working prototypes, often through partnerships with the AT&T Foundry, AT&T Labs, or outreach efforts. TIP then positions these ideas for commercialization within an AT&T business unit.

---

18 Lydia Dishman, "How Inome's $100k Cash Prize Encourages Employees To Innovate Like Entrepreneurs," *Fast Company*, July 3, 2012, http://www.fastcompany.com/1841906/how-inomes-100k-cash-prize-encourages-employees-innovate-entrepreneurs.

The beauty of TIP is that the crowd (made up of AT&T employees) decides which ideas they think will be successful, based on their votes and comments during the TIP process. After ideas rise to the top, the founders have the opportunity to build business proposals and develop use cases before pitching their ideas to an Angel committee made up of AT&T senior executives for funding. It's a truly collaborative model that takes into account feedback from the entire employee base to ensure great ideas are seen.

According to Douglas S. Ring, director of construction and engineering, AT&T, TIP is successful when employees are driven to participate in the innovation process and are creating products and services that are meaningful to customers and business.

"Our focus is always about innovating for our customers," said Ring. "We monitor how active our employees are on TIP and are always looking for new opportunities to involve them in the program. For example, TIP implements innovation challenges for employees issued by AT&T leaders. These challenges range from business units across the company and are designed to address a specific need or goal. If we're able to develop a solution to a specific business need, we know our TIP process has been successful."

Since TIP's inception, AT&T has allocated $44 million to fund new ideas. TIP is open to all employees at AT&T. Today, the program has more than 130,000 members from all 50 states and 54 countries. More than 31,000 ideas have been submitted into the TIP community with dozens developed and successfully launched.[19]

Creation and curation of an ideator: Ring's story

One idea that rose through the ranks was AT&T Toggle, created by Ring himself, who formulated the idea while struggling with a question familiar to many of us: How do I keep my work life separate from my

---

19 These and subsequent insights from Douglas S. Ring are from an email interview with the authors in February 2015.

private life on my phone? He imagined creating two versions of his phone; each would be walled off from the other side.

"I was working my normal day job in network operations and the idea for AT&T Toggle came out of my own personal frustrations of trying to keep my work phone separate from my personal life," Ring explained. "I submitted the idea for AT&T Toggle and people started rallying and collaborating around it. I was surprised to find out my idea had risen in popularity because in my mind, I was just trying to think of a solution for my personal frustrations."

Notice that Ring didn't necessarily consider himself an ideator. But, with a defined outlet and strong encouragement from others, he realized that his ideas can have true market value. We were intrigued by this story and decided to go straight to Ring himself to further explain the process that got him thinking and kept him engaged. Here's what he had to say.

IGNITE Authors: How did you become an innovator?

Ring: I believe innovation happens when people get excited about solving a problem to the point that they take action and work toward solving that problem. I know that's perhaps overly broad; However, I believe that when we think of it this way, we are very inclusive of those that may otherwise not consider themselves innovators. When we tell people this is the definition of innovation then we invite them into the process and our idea pool expands.

In my case, TIP invited me to get excited about something I was passionate about and then they enabled me to work on the 'problem' or idea that I had despite not being in a product development organization.

IGNITE Authors: What's the biggest challenge to overcome when presenting an idea?

Ring: I believe a person's biggest challenge can be how the innovation program at their corporation is structured. Fortunately, here at AT&T, we have developed a mature process through TIP.

[Once the idea gets the green light], though, it likely comes down to the person's confidence level, willingness to collaborate versus going it alone, and accepting and embracing critical feedback that would improve the idea, and building strong support amongst others who share the same 'problem.' The support will help the idea submitter to validate the problem and perhaps expand on the solution. Later in the innovation process, these supporters will likely be key to voting on the project passing to the next decision gate.

However, I believe not all ideas are created equal. In my opinion, corporations are in search of the next billion-dollar product. So the challenge is to come up with that next killer idea.

IGNITE Authors: Has your idea been successful? How do you know?

Ring: I had a small team of collaborators that gathered to improve the idea I submitted. We passed through several decision gates until we were awarded funding to develop a proof of concept idea for further consideration. We ultimately presented the idea to our Chairman and CEO Randal Stephenson and a business unit picked it up and turned it into a product. We also received United States Patent 8,699,413 in April of 2014. We're all very pleased and humbled to see our efforts resulting in a successful AT&T product.

IGNITE Authors: Do you continue to be involved in the innovation process at AT&T?

Ring: At the time of my idea submission, I was an employee who had an idea, got excited, took the initiative to submit the idea, and saw it through until the end. In my current capacity, I remain an interested party in the TIP process. If I feel I have a killer idea, I'm likely to submit it. When time permits, I like to review ideas that are submitted and offer feedback and "vote the idea up" through one of the collaboration tools available on our TIP site. Because of my success with AT&T Toggle, I am approached on occasion for advice by others who are in the pitch phase.

IGNITE Authors: How did you prove your idea would work before launching it? A pilot program?

Ring: Before we were given funding to develop AT&T Toggle, we put together a business plan and presented that to an Angel committee (a group of AT&T executives). From there, we assembled a small team of internal coders and developers to agilely develop a proof of concept, which was demonstrated to different areas within the business before it landed within a business area for further development and productization.

Stating the case for creating an innovative culture and for seeking out intrapreneurs, like Ring, to help push that innovation forward is just the starting point. To genuinely get value out of this kind of a venture, you must be prepared to make the investment in retaining the best talent and sustaining the forward momentum. Are you ready?

Chapter 4:
How to Keep Innovative Employees (and Employees Innovative)

Not long ago, global consulting firm Accenture conducted an eye-opening study on innovation among more than 500 U.S., U.K., and French executives. At the time, an overwhelming 70 percent of survey respondents considered innovation at least among the top five strategic priorities at their companies, and two-thirds of those executives said they're extremely or very dependent on innovation for long-term success.

But here's the kicker: Only *18 percent* said they had actually realized a competitive advantage from their innovation strategies.[1] The study went on to conclude the major cause of this discrepancy stems from risk aversion. This penchant for low risk results in an overly cautious, painstakingly incremental approach to innovation that, quite simply, doesn't work. According to the study:

1 An overview of the Accenture study can be found here: Chris Murphy, "*Innovation Isn't Working at 4 out of 5 Companies*," *InformationWeek Government*, May 16, 2013, http://www.informationweek.com/it-leadership/innovation-isnt-working-at-4-out-of-5-companies/d/d-id/1109987.

"By putting formal systems in place to manage innovation, companies can protect themselves from such risk. Enterprises able to successfully innovate at a breakthrough level are far more likely to dominate and prosper in the new markets they create. They can also position themselves to master change."[2]

Starting an innovation and ideation program in your workplace can have many positive effects for your employees, from product development, to increased profits, to better retention. But, like any other business endeavor, it needs a solid-yet-aggressive framework to succeed. Most of these programs have great intentions but the signal gets lost in the noise when it comes to effectively reaching employees. When this happens, employees who might have joined your organization, or have stayed with your organization, are quickly discouraged.

To illustrate these additional forces working against you, consider this: A study by Millennial Branding and Monster.com found that less than one-third of workers feel they have the freedom, flexibility, and resources to be an intrapreneur.[3]

Innovation Exists in Another Dimension

The foundation for building out the IGNITE Framework is a full pipeline of intrapreneurs working in your organization. Otherwise, you may fall prey to a classic scenario we shared in our first book *The Future of Nonprofits: Thrive and Innovate in the Digital Age*. These days, nonprofits hire smart people in their 20's and 30's for their ideas.

"Let's try this new way to fundraise using social media." Or, "What if we built an app to better schedule our volunteer drivers over the holidays?"

Nonprofits proceed by saying "NO" to all these ideas.

---

2 Accenture Report, "Why 'Low Risk' Innovation is Costly: Overcoming the Perils of Renovation and Invention," accessed December 4, 2015, http://www.cas-americas.com/us-en/Pages/insight-low-risk-innovation-costly.aspx.
3 Dan Schawbel, "3 Things You Didn't Know About Intrapreneurship," *Entrepreneur*, September 3, 2013, http://www.entrepreneur.com/article/227725.

Finally, the nonprofits wonder why these young professionals with great ideas quickly leave.[4]

Having an innovation program like the IGNITE Framework in play at your organization can be a multiplier of employee retention across levels, from your most junior employee to your most senior. Your frontline junior employee—whether they are on the floor selling or at your customer service center answering emails—will appreciate an innovation program, as it lets them express their creative freedom through their ideas. Your senior employees—whether they are in team management or at the executive or chief level—will appreciate an innovation program as a way to mentor employees, move great ideas into production, and retain innovative thinkers. And, for those senior innovative employees, it might even be a source of revenue.

A senior vice president at the hosting company Rackspace told us of a company called HelpSocial that started as an idea inside the company, but has since been successfully spun out as its own company. Now that same VP that led development has a seat on the startup's Board of Directors. A very innovative model indeed.

Fellow innovation expert Mitch Ditkoff, co-founder and president of Idea Champions, has said, "Real innovation doesn't happen on paper. It happens in another dimension—the human dimension—the realm of authentic interaction, not theoretical interfacing."[5]

Amen to that. Ditkoff published a list of 20 things a company needs to do when interfacing with innovative employees to keep them interested enough to stop updating their LinkedIn profiles. We agree so much with this list that we've included the top five here.

---

4 David J. Neff and Randal C. Moss, *The Future of Nonprofits: Innovate and Thrive in the Digital Age* (New Jersey: Wiley, 2011).
5 Mitch Ditkoff, "20 Ways to Spark Innovation in Others," *HuffPost Business*, June 11, 2013, http://www.huffingtonpost.com/mitch-ditkoff/how-to-spark-innovation-i_b_3421992.html.

1. **Be curious.**

    One thing is certain: Aspiring innovators are on to something. If you are interested in increasing an innovator's odds of success, your first task is to find out *what*, precisely, has captured their attention. Curiosity may have killed the cat, but it greatly enlivens the person on the brink of a new possibility.

2. **Listen deeply.**

    People with a new idea often need to express what they're thinking in order to fully understand what they're conjuring. *Listening* is the main way you can help—not so you'll have something wise to say in response, but so you can create a safe haven for others to explore the nuances of their new ideas.

3. **Ask powerful questions.**

    You may be someone's boss, or have multiple degrees, but that doesn't mean you have all the answers. Indeed, when it comes to sparking innovation, *asking questions*—at the right time and in the right way—is more important than giving advice. It is often the only thing you need to do.

4. **Reframe the challenge.**

    As an innovation catalyst, one of the biggest contributions you can make is to ensure that the innovators in your life have clearly defined their projects. Probe. Poke. Pester. See if there is another, more elegant, way they can define their goal—starting with the words, "How can I?"

5. **Eliminate bureaucratic obstacles.**

    Innovators have enough to worry about without having to navigate the often Rube Goldberg-like maze of corporate systems and the ever-changing marketplace. Be their advocate.

Demystify the roadblocks. Identify what's in their way and do what you can to eliminate the obstacles.

Ditkoff goes on to list 15 more habits that can help in managing innovators: provide resources, coach, give feedback, hit pause, lean in when necessary, celebrate small wins, reinforce the vision of success, and tell inspiring stories. Additional habits are to quote from the innovation masters (he recommends reading the LEGO Group's *Less Management, More Orchestrating*), model the spirit of innovation, decrease the fear of failure, and more.[6]

As you read through the list, what attributes do you recognize in yourself as you manage your regular employees? How about your all-star employees? Wait: You don't manage those two groups in the same way? That's okay. You shouldn't. What we want you to understand in this chapter is not how to manage the bulk of your employees. Go read some classic Drucker for that. Instead, we want to keep you focused on how to keep innovative employees and keep employees innovative. As you can see from most of Ditkoff's points, challenging and motivating intrapreneurs is a whole different ballgame.

Now, as business owners and executives, do we reward loyal employees to stay the course, or is jumping ship the way to get ahead? And, if it's the latter, is this a business model for success or failure?

Recognize and Reward Innovative DNA

Janine Popick is the former CEO of the marketing company VerticalResponse, located in the San Francisco Bay Area. When she considers employee retention for innovative thinkers, it all boils down to a couple of factors regarding the level of innovation within an organization.

---

6 If you're interested in reading more about these and other tips from Ditkoff, we recommend visiting his website at www.ideachampions.com.

In her opinion, "Creating an environment where employees feel a strong connection to the work they do and having a positive work environment has never been more important. How does that translate for your business? It depends, but could include flexible work arrangements like working at home, or working a flexible schedule. You have to examine the DNA of your organization and find out what's of value to your team so you can create that environment in genuine and sincere ways that matter to the people who make it tick."[7]

Here's a bit of modern folklore that serves as an example of innovative DNA in action. This story is an excerpt from William J. Powers' 2014 State of the University Address at the University of Texas at Austin:

> *Herb Kelleher, former chairman and CEO of Southwest Airlines, wanted gate agents to take more initiative. For example, if an incoming plane was late, should they hold the connecting flights, risking further problems downstream? Or should they send them, risking stranding incoming passengers? Herb wanted the gate agent to decide, not to be paralyzed until someone higher up decided.*

> *A flight destined for Long Island was forced to divert to Baltimore because of bad weather. It was late, and there were no more flights departing for the night. The youngest, most junior agent — who was still a probationary employee — had to deal with the stranded customers. She chartered three buses to transport the customers to Long Island so they could sleep in their own beds that night — without regard for the expense to the airline.*

> *She was summoned to Dallas, which probably made her a bit apprehensive. But when she arrived at the corporate headquarters, she discovered she was the guest of honor at a party just for her. Herb Kelleher celebrated her decisiveness, her courage, and her heart. He wanted everyone else to be more like her. She took a risk — and Herb backed her.*

---

7 Janine Popick, "Why Employees Stay (and Why They Go)," *Inc.*, June 7, 2013, http://www.inc.com/janine-popick/why-employees-stay-and-why-they-go.html?nav=featured.

We need to be more like Herb Kelleher. Sometimes you have to take risks to get the job done right. We won't get innovation if everyone is afraid of getting slapped every time an experiment in innovation doesn't work.[8]

Take, for example, Michael Lewis, the founder and CEO of Forever Collectibles, a premier manufacturer of officially licensed sports and novelty products. A few short years ago, according to *Inc.com*, a young staffer suggested that the company, which makes sports-related baubles officially licensed by all the major college and pro sports associations, should start selling sports-themed ugly sweaters. But Lewis was beyond skeptical. He wasn't aware that thousands, if not hundreds of thousands, of people wore them for fun or as part of holiday parties.

One year later, the company realized $10 million in ugly sweater sales.[9]

This success was achieved because Lewis did two things. First, he recognized a trend and, second, he listened to an employee who was challenging the status quo at his company. But there's more to the story than that. As *Inc.com* asks in the article, "What was it about sweaters, in particular, that caused Lewis to second-guess the boldness with which he usually embraced new ideas?"

That's where we stumble upon the real lessons behind these ugly sweaters.

While Lewis has a background in apparel, his company was set up to license and make everything but apparel. He knew that the giants that lived in the apparel industry might have already had this idea. Nike, Adidas, and Reebok are experts at apparel. Lewis's company was not. Sure, Forever Collectibles might be able to make a sweater or two. But really launching this side of the business—creating, marketing, and keeping it going, especially against someone like Nike—was an entirely different story.

---

8 As of September 2015, the full State of the University Address could be found here: http://www.utexas.edu/faculty/council/2014-2015/reports/university_address.pdf.
9 Ilan Mochari, "How My Employees Helped Me Make $10 Million Selling Ugly Christmas Sweaters," *Inc.*, December 18, 2014, http://www.inc.com/ilan-mochari/ugly-sweaters.html.

Then there was the design challenge. As our co-author David knows, an ugly sweater has to be *ugly*. (David has thrown a Mustache and Bad Sweater Party that doubles as a benefit party for the nonprofit Movember for the past 6 years, as referenced in the photo here.)[10]

Meanwhile, licensors like the University of Texas or the Dallas Cowboys want their products to be anything BUT ugly. As *Inc.com* points out, "So much of Forever Collectibles' competitive advantage stems from its ability to make money for pro and college licensing offices. The last thing Lewis would want is for the licensors to become skeptical about his company's ability to deliver sales on a new product. A flop had the potential to hurt Forever Collectibles' reputation with its results-oriented partners."

Despite all of this, his employees persuaded him to reserve judgement. Instead, they created a design and, in the miracle of modern manufacturing, had it sent to China to create a sample. In less than 48 hours, a sweater was in Lewis's hands.

Once he had the product in his hands, his other concerns started to fall away. He took the samples and brought them to the colleges and licensees. They liked what they saw. Next came more samples to convince more people, and marketplace research. The findings? None of the "big boys" were doing this. Then came an entrepreneurial epiphany: He didn't need to make 3 million of these. Instead, he would control the supply and make limited-edition ugly sweaters only. The strange thing? Rumor has it that the company's medium sizes were in such short supply that they started re-selling online for $120 to $180 (two to three times the original retail price).

Are you ready to let your employees change your mind? Have you already shot them down?

Take Intrapreneurs "Off the Leash"

Having an innovation program or an idea lab at your business is a major part of this. And, along those lines, the basics of the IGNITE Framework can help you retain the best among your employees.

We are also firm believers in presenting people with opportunities to learn. This is especially true with intrapreneurs. Don't just provide these innovative employees with your average training and professional development opportunities such as selling techniques 101, time and expense reporting 201, or community involvement basics. Don't simply subject them to your boring, standard compliance training that happens once every two years. Instead, allow them a budget and a scholarship procedure to attend industry events.

Taking your intrapreneurs "off the leash" and giving them open range outside the confines of your organization is one of the most motivating things you can do. Be sure to encourage them to not just attend events, but to speak at the events, arrive early or stay late for networking opportunities, to make friends, andt to exchange ideas. Encouraging the intrapreneurs among your ranks to become thought leaders can pay off for your brand in ways you never expected.

Thought leadership can benefit your organization in the following three ways.

1. Sowing the seeds.

A good employee simply attends a conference to speak and then leaves as soon as possible after speaking. A great employee, the kind you want to keep around, attends before and after their speaking gig. They map out the most relevant panels, meet-ups and sessions to attend. They take notes of new and original content and ideas they hear about. When David attended SXSW in 2009 he went to an interesting panel about user-generated content by the "Ask a Ninja" video series and podcast creators. One speaker reflected on his usage of creative commons for materials and how the more content he put out, the more his audience not just consumed it (the classic 90 percent rule of community[11]) but, instead, re-mixed it and made it their own. This inspired David to go back and submit a Futuring and Innovation grant application at the American Cancer Society for Sharinghope.TV, which became the first user-generated content community for cancer survivors in the world.

2. Online networking.

This one is simple. The business card is not dead; it should be collected and curated. Our network of choice for this is LinkedIn. After a speaking session, there is usually a line of people eager to ask questions, follow up, or even pitch what they are working on. Or the speaker may be asked for a job. We have seen it all. As audience members come up and speak to your intrapreneur, encourage them to collect business cards and then follow up on LinkedIn, indicating the connection where they met. This has enabled Randal to find specific technology vendors in the past as well as other speaking opportunities.

3. Pressing the flesh.

Take the leap and become an expert at face-to-face networking. After spending 6-7 straight hours attending lectures, listening to keynotes and enjoying rubber-chicken dinners, we understand your desire to get back to your room. However, the real networking during thought leadership events is done after hours (or after the presentations). Encourage intrapreneurs to save energy for these activities.

---

11 Dr. Michael Wu, Ph.D., "The 90-9-1 Rule in Reality," *Lithium's Science of Social blog*, September 14, 2012, http://community.lithium.com/t5/Science-of-Social-blog/The-90-9-1-Rule-in-Reality/ba-p/5463.

That being said, here are some of our favorite events to attend in the digital strategy world. Your results may vary.

- **SXSW:** A must for all innovators. SXSW is a week's worth of panels, meet-ups, keynotes, parties, and more packed into the streets of Austin, TX. Over 80,000 people attend each year to learn more about technology, digital strategy, innovation, film, and music.

- **NTEN's NTC:** The national nonprofit technology conference brings together several thousand nonprofit technology folks for panels, keynotes, volunteering, meetups, beer socials, and parties. We tend to think it could be interesting for our for-profit friends as well. Everything from panels on digital currency to best practices for email conversion.

- **POP TECH:** This conference brings together over 600 thinkers and doers from around the world to share projects and ideas. It's in its 20th year and takes place in Camden, Maine. The conference hosts a wide variety of tech folks. With big thinkers and electrifying speakers, the event is an ideal environment to generate ideas and explore the possibilities.

- **TED and TEDx TALKS:** While the TED brand is starting to waver a bit (it can vary from city to city, depending on the organizers and the format they follow), it's a great place to gain inspiration from a wide variety of topics. From how stand-up comedy improves your life (from our very own David J. Neff at TEDx Houston) to physicists talking about string theory, there's something inspiring to be found at almost every event.

Provide a Supporting Structure

Again, when it comes to keeping your employees innovative and keeping innovative employees, it boils down to structure. Do you have the necessary governance and structure in place to keep an innovation program up and running and successful year after year? Are the leaders of your company ready to make this happen? In *The 2020 Workplace*,[12] Jeanne C. Meister and Karie Willyerd define what the leaders of the year 2020 will look like.

They've given us permission to share with you the following visual:[13]

The 2020 Leader
Being this kind of leader... requires these management behaviors

Collaborative Mind-set	• Inclusive decision making • Genuine solicitation of feedback
Developer of People	• Mentors and coaches team • Provides straight feedback
Digitally Confident	• Uses technology to connect to customers and employees
Global Citizen	• Has a diverse mind-set • Prioritizes social responsibility
Anticipates and Builds for the Future	• Builds accountability across levels • Champions innovation

www.futureworkplace.com

Take a look across the five attributes they list. While all five categories are strong points, leaders who exhibit a collaborative mind-set and those who anticipate and build for the future exhibit two core attributes we see reflected back to us in our IGNITE Framework.

---

12 Jeanne C. Meister and Karie Willyerd, *The 2020 Workplace: How Innovative Companies Attract, Develop, and Keep Tomorrow's Employees Today* (New York: HarperCollins, 2010).
13 This image is published with special permission and is owned and copyrighted by Future Workplace. Find out more at www.futureworkplace.com.

In fact, these two core attributes remind us of an intrapreneur we know named Jason Shim. Shim is the an associate director of digital strategy and alumni relations for the nonprofit Pathways to Education Canada. He took these two values to heart when he decided the nonprofit should explore taking the cryptocurrency known as Bitcoin as a donation option. If you are not familiar with Bitcoin, Shim defines it as an open source digital peer-to-peer currency. It was released in 2009 and is based on an algorithm that regulates the amount of currency available and confirms transactions.

What Shim found compelling about the currency is that it allows individuals and organizations to exchange units of value without a central authority. We see it as one of the new methods of digital currency that could be defining our future, but that's another book. To get his nonprofit to experiment with something like Bitcoin, Shim had to work collaboratively with his fundraising department.

Why did he put so much effort into such a unique concept? He anticipated that it would be important to the future of his organization. Both of those ideas line up with the system of attributes described by Meister and Willyerd.

To gain a better understanding of these leadership attributes and the process that can take their ideas and turn them into business success, we interviewed Shim about his innovation around Bitcoin. This is what he had to say.

IGNITE Authors: What was your big idea pertaining to cryptocurrency at your nonprofit?

Shim: The big idea around cryptocurrency at Pathways to Education Canada was to set up the infrastructure and processes to accept Bitcoin and to issue receipts for income tax purposes. There were people who were chatting on forums about wanting to donate Bitcoin to charities, but there weren't a lot of charities that were accepting Bitcoin in 2013.

IGNITE Authors: What was your strategy to get the idea into practice?

Shim: Before presenting my idea, it was important to gather as much research as possible about Bitcoin and its viability in a nonprofit environment. I wanted to ensure that I could address any questions that would be raised, so I looked up a couple of charities—one in Nova Scotia, and the other in New York—that had implemented Bitcoin donations on their websites. I also had a conversation with the folks at Archive.org about their experience. They provided some great help by sharing their experience and providing a few suggestions. However, none of these organizations issued tax receipts for Bitcoin donations, so I reviewed some of the guidance that had been issued by the Canada Revenue Agency (The Canadian equivalent of the American IRS) and called them directly to get some clarity around how they would treat Bitcoin donations.

After compiling all the research, I set up a meeting with some of the members of our finance and fundraising teams at our organization and presented them with a two-page briefing outlining the opportunity and the benefits. I was also very clear about identifying potential risks and how they would be mitigated. The team provided great initial feedback and, from there, I [presented it] at an all-staff meeting to introduce Bitcoin to everyone in the organization. I then spent a couple days sorting out the technical implementation pieces and we were done.

IGNITE Authors: When you presented your idea, what was the biggest challenge you had to overcome?

Shim: At the time, Bitcoin was in the news quite a bit and the biggest challenge to overcome was cutting through all the media sensationalism and providing a space for people to look at it objectively.

IGNITE Authors: How did you prove your idea would work before launching it? A pilot program?

Shim: Overall, the program was considered a pilot. It also helped that there was a fund called the Bitcoin100 that donated $1,000 to charities that adopted Bitcoin, so there was already a donation waiting as soon as we launched. I also secured a $500 donation from a local Bitcoin exchange. The assurance of $1,500 in donations upon launching helped to validate the idea.

IGNITE Authors: How did management react to the idea?

Shim: They were open and receptive to the idea, which I appreciated. As I mentioned previously, there was a lot of media sensationalism around Bitcoin at the time, but they took the time to understand how it could benefit the organization.

IGNITE Authors: Has your idea been successful? How do you know?

Shim: Yes. We have received over $2,300 in donations to-date since implementing Bitcoin donations. In addition, I have had the opportunity to provide advice and support to numerous other charities in the U.S. and Canada who have also implemented Bitcoin donations.[14]

Again, we see research and collaboration intertwined with entrepreneurial drive behind Shim getting Bitcoin implemented at his nonprofit.

Setting Up the Environment

You may have noticed by now an oft-repeated motif around the concept of innovation labs. We'll talk more about innovation labs throughout the book but, for now, let's examine how labs can make or break an intrapreneur-friendly environment. Specifically, are labs a benefit to just those who get to be a part of the lab? Do they push those employees not involved to aspirationally hope they could one day be a part of the lab?

We know that innovation works best when there is a dedicated set of resources to make it happen. Whether it is a physical location or a corner of the corporate intranet, carving out a space helps engaged participants feel special, which engenders commitment.

FirstBuild is such a space. This collaboration between GE Appliance and Local Motors is a microfactory built exclusively for the development and testing of new collaboratively sourced innovative solutions.[15] A space completely separate from the GE manufacturing facility, on the University of Louisville campus, FirstBuild is on the vanguard of collaborative innovation. It attracts engineers, scientists, early adopters, industrial designers, and makers in an attempt to identify and create the next generation of appliances.

The space and its programs engage GE Appliance employees to realize solutions suggested and developed by a community of makers and appliance

---

14 These comments by Jason Shim are from an email interview with the authors, January 18, 2015.
15 See the FirstBuild website, accessed December 5, 2015, https://firstbuild.com/about.

enthusiasts. In this unique environment, GE Appliance employees get a unique experience that allows them to quickly explore concept ideas, and develop into the leaders of the future.

Amazon's Lab126 is reported to be the company's R&D unit with offices in Sunnyvale and Cupertino, California. Lab126 is run by Gregg Zehr, a former Apple vice president with a mellow vibe who plays guitar and has a flair for classic style. According to an article in *Fast Company*, "He'd wear a tweed jacket and a scarf at the lab, and it never looked weird." Former Lab126 Vice President Mark Randall recalls, "When I walked into his house for the first time, I said, 'Jesus Christ, Gregg, this looks like an Apple store.'"[16]

Amazon is a company that strives to make big, bold leaps forward. And Lab126 specializes in that kind of boldness. According to *Fast Company*:

> *"Each 'science experiment,' as those inside the lab describe their projects, is labeled with a letter of the alphabet. (Indeed, Lab126's name itself is a play on A to Z, with 1 representing the first letter of the alphabet and 26 the last.) These experiments evolved over years of development into a hardware portfolio that now includes Amazon's Fire TV set-top box and the new Echo, a sort of Siri-in-a-tube that's engineered to answer any spoken question. Many other projects will likely never come to market, such as Project C, imagined as an experimental device for the home that would project a display screen onto any surface and allow users to interact with it through gestures.*

This particular lab does have its downfalls. According to the article, very few employees have access to it. "If you really wanted to peek in, you could crouch down and look through the bottom of the (frosted) window," joked one source according to *Fast Company*.

Of course, late in 2015, *The New York Times* released a damning report of Amazon culture overall, saying that it is a bruising, tear-inducing workplace

---

16 Austin Carr, "The Real Story Behind Jeff Bezos's Fire Phone Debacle and What It Means for Amazon's Future," *Fast Company*, January 6, 2015, http://www.fastcompany.com/3039887/under-fire.

that chews up and spits out white collar workers at a surprising pace.[17] According to the Lab126 website they are huge believers in this culture and the famous Amazon Leadership Principles that allegedly fuel this behavior at the company.[18] (Then again, there are two sides to every story, including an article from *Wired* that claimed "Amazon employees who complained about the work-life balance at the company actually tended to give Amazon a higher rating."[19])

When it comes to the idea of Skunk Works and labs, are these processes simply building ivory towers that only a select group of employees can be a part of? Do these kinds of selective and secretive operations make use of the collective intelligence in an organization or do they breed contempt from those who never get the opportunity to engage with them?

We value the open labs concept for its ability to launch game-changing outputs, and the excitement it can generate in employees. We also understand the desire to keep innovation development secret, much to our chagrin. There is value in running a dual system that leverages both the selective and discrete nature of a Skunk Works program and the broad engagement of an open innovation initiative. In a truly innovative company, there is room for both a closed lab and an IGNITE-powered open innovation system. In this book, we'll describe how an open IGNITE Framework system could serve as a single point of intake, while specific concepts may be routed into a closed-lab program to get further developed based on criteria set by the organization.

It's OK to Bring in Reinforcements

In November 2015 alone, $9.73 billion in funding flowed from venture investors to 832 startups, an increase of almost $2 billion from the month

---

17 Jodi Kantor and David Streitfeld, "Inside Amazon: Wrestling Big Ideas in a Bruising Workplace," *The New York Times*, August 15, 2015, http://www.nytimes.com/2015/08/16/technology/inside-amazon-wrestling-big-ideas-in-a-bruising-workplace.html?_r=0.
18 Amazon's "Our Leadership Prinicples," accessed December 5, 2015, https://www.amazon.jobs/principles.
19 Davey Alba, "Amazonians Who Have to Work Too Much Like Amazon More," *Wired*, August 20, 2015, http://www.wired.com/2015/08/amazonians-work-much-like-amazon/.

prior.[20] That is a monumental amount and, perhaps, proof that sometimes innovative groups just need to be found outside of existing organizations. For instance, the Walt Disney Company holds annual startup funding competitions (powered by the folks at TechStars) during which they give seed money and access to Disney executives for coaching and mentorship.[21] The startups get funding and support while Disney gets insights and inspiration that they can use internally to fuel future strategic growth.

Innovation by nature is exciting and exhilarating work. Taking an inclusive approach and bringing as many people into the processes as possible is preferred. At some point, though, you will need individuals to become deeper and more prolific contributors, managing the review process and helping newly funded innovators through the development journey. The next chapter will explore how to effectively identify the skills, personalities, and experience you will need in your review team.

20 Mikey Tom, "VC Snapshot: November," *PitchBook News & Analysis* (on the company's website), December 4, 2015, http://pitchbook.com/4Q_2014.html.
21 Max Taves, "F-U-N-D-E-D: Eyeing Innovation, Disney Sees Big Future in the Tiny Companies," *CNET*, July 10, 2015, http://www.cnet.com/news/funded-eyeing-innovation-disney-sees-big-future-in-tiny-companies/.

Chapter 5:
Assembling Your
Innovation Team

"I love it when a plan comes together."

—Col. John "Hannibal" Smith from the
NBC television series "The A-Team"

Between 1983 and 1987, Americans were treated to the televised heroics (and antics) of a band of vigilante ex-U.S. Special Forces soldiers fighting for the rights of the oppressed. This, of course, was The A-Team.

Led by the always-unorthodox Colonel John "Hannibal" Smith (George Peppard), the team included Lieutenant Templeton "Faceman" Peck, a smooth-talking conman (Dirk Benedict); Captain H.M. "Howling Mad" Murdock, who was declared insane and lived in a mental institution (Dwight Schultz); and Sergeant First Class Bosco "B.A.," or "Bad Attitude," Baracus, the team's strong man and mechanic (played by the inimitable Mr. T).

In hindsight, each episode was as predictable as the sunrise. Someone is in trouble and needs help. Somehow they summon The A-Team to their aid.

Conflict and inevitable confrontation is followed by a monumental project and an eventual resolution via gratuitous explosions.

While the plot was predictable, it was also satisfying. Why? The brilliance was in the team dynamic. The seemingly dysfunctional group dynamic that was the source of their perpetual hijinks was also the source of their continued success. In fact, their success is the ongoing punchline to the joke, "A cunning strategist, a conman, a mentally unstable pilot, and a brutish mechanic walk into a bar. What happens?" (If you're wondering, the punch line is, "Millions of dollars.")

What made The A-Team so successful was that seemingly odd mix of personalities, skill sets, life experiences, personal interest, and professional backgrounds. Every single member of the team brings a unique hand of cards to the table. Sure, they're fictional personas, written to bring a unique blend to the screen. Intentionally hyperbolic? Absolutely. Completely unreplicable? Not necessarily.

A Study of A-Team Dynamics (Seriously)

With the help of Wikipedia,[1] let's look at the profiles of each member of The A-Team independently, through a more critical and business-like lens. Trust us. It'll be worth your time.

Colonel John "Hannibal" Smith:

Hannibal is distinguished by his unflappable demeanor, even when in peril. Thriving on adventure and the adrenaline rush of life-threatening situations, he seems to genuinely enjoy every challenge the team encounters. Hannibal is renowned by both allies and enemies for being cool-headed and extremely clever. There is rarely a situation in which he is not able to smile in the face of adversity. He is a master tactician, although his plans rarely turn out as planned.

---

1 "The A-Team," *Wikipedia*, accessed December 5, 2015, http://en.wikipedia.org/wiki/The_A-Team.

In business terms, Hannibal is a natural-born leader. He is cool under pressure, with a proven track record for achieving success. Moreover, he is someone who actively seeks out confrontation and thrives on overcoming challenges. He's a flexible leader who has the ability to pivot and redirect resources when plans do not materialize, yet he still manages to achieve key goals and milestones.

Lieutenant Templeton "Faceman" Peck

Suave and smooth-talking, Face (as the team calls him) serves as the team's con man and scrounger, able to get his hands on just about anything they need. He arranges for supplies, equipment, and sensitive information using numerous scams and hustles. When Hannibal is elsewhere or captured, Face often takes the helm of the team. He usually organizes the fees for their services, due to his aptitude with numbers, and at times is shown to have the ability to count large amounts of money or value expensive items within a matter of seconds. Face is the gentlest member of the team, generally attempting to avoid conflict.

In business terms, Face is a cunning and adept resource manager. He is able to identify key components and acquire them while simultaneously managing the bottom line of the enterprise. He is a keen quartermaster and is also savvy with intelligence and information gathering. Face is an aspiring leader and has the interests and personality to engage executives in both business and highly cultural conversations.

Captain H. M. "Howling Mad" Murdock

Considered the best chopper pilot of the Vietnam War, Murdock was officially declared insane (possibly caused by post-traumatic stress disorder). He is intuitively capable of flying anything with rotors or wings, including passenger planes, fighter jets, and even autogyros. Murdock earned three unit citations and a Silver Star. He actually has extensive knowledge of various subjects and keeps up on current events, showing a genius-level aptitude. He speaks several languages including Spanish, German, Vietnamese, Japanese, Russian, and Mandarin Chinese. He also seems to possess a photographic memory.

In business terms, Murdock is a specialist. His avionics expertise is invaluable to the team. His proficiency with foreign languages makes him an asset when collaborating globally. His ability to recount project details without referencing material that may be inaccessible is essentially important. Murdock has honed his quick decision making skills over the years as a pilot, able to work with multiple tools as represented by proficiency in both rotary and fixed winged aircraft. But working with people? He'll leave that to the more charismatic members of the team.

Sergeant First Class Bosco Albert "B.A." (Bad Attitude) Baracus

This man is a mechanical genius. He also has one of the worst conduct records in the U.S. Army. A rough-and-tough fighter, B.A.'s confrontational attitude usually leads to a more direct approach to problem solving, which often involve either his skills at hand-to-hand combat or his mechanics. He possesses a talent for making impressive machinery out of just about any ordinary parts. Despite B.A.'s reputed attitude, he is a kind person who has a special fondness for children, occasionally working at a youth center teaching sports to kids. He suffers from pteromechanophobia, an intense fear of flying.

In business terms, B.A. is a master maker, which means he's able to improvise physical creations with limited resources. He showcases his skills in mechanical engineering by fashioning one-off solutions to fulfill the strategies set out by his team leader. A natural born negotiator, B.A. is able to set a distinct line during tense negotiations and stand ground on the tough choices, using a strong moral compass.

***

The mixture is the magic here. Each team member is above average in their own right. But when their varied backgrounds, skills, and experiences are combined, the potential is even larger than the sum of its parts—even when it doesn't seem like the pieces will fit. In fact, vast deviation from the formula would conceivably lead to a less effective team. Subtract the pilot and add an extra scavenger and the group transforms into an immobile and suspect lot.

This team chemistry is important for every team, particularly when building a support structure for an innovation program. In fact, team chemistry just may be the key to your innovation program's success. Picking the right people with the right skill sets is one of the most important initial decisions you will make.

Your innovation team will be reviewing, allotting funds, and coaching the innovators. Their team dynamics affect the success of the innovations you are developing every bit as much as the project manager and the quality of the idea itself. Like any support network, the work functions and personalities of your team members have to be varied yet specific. Sound impossible? It's not. Pull apart these two elements and you'll see how.

Importance of Work Functions

This area represents the explicit job functions and job skills that inevitably appear on an official job description. In other words, it's how you'd describe your job to your mother. You may be an accountant, marketer, research associate, graphic designer, or in IT. But what do you DO? You count, divide, sell, design, and position things. Are these things just as important as a job title? Absolutely. It's what your company hired you to do. It is your job.

One of the most difficult things for a professional to accomplish is to self-assess work functions. More often than not, they will downplay or short-change themselves. Like writing your own resume, assessing one's own work functions requires a third-person view of what you actually do in a day, week, month, and year. We once talked with an accountant who told us her work function was "accounting." When we began to talk with her about her daily grind she began to realize that her work function involved so much more. Beyond simply accounting she was managing external vendor relationships (accounting firms), managing risk (financial reports and recommendations), and even handling human resource management (managing her interns).

Truly understanding the work functions of each team member is critical to building an innovation team. Do not overlook the intricacies of work functions because it is this minutia that could provide the greatest value— or the greatest stumbling block—in the most critical moments.

It's then important to incorporate a balance of key work functions across your team members. This is crucial because, throughout the innovation development process, you will need expertise across all areas. Oftentimes innovators (those individuals sending you their brilliant ideas) lack the business development and management experience necessary to take an innovation from idea to implementation. This is where having a team with varied and practical work skills can make or break the innovation itself.

Innovation development is like a microcosm of your corporation. And so it stands to reason that you will want to have all of the major functional areas represented on your team. A great starting lineup would include representatives from legal, accounting or finance, sales/business development, marketing, IT, and operations. It is as if you are assembling the key skill sets to launch your own company. In fact, the more you think of it in those terms, the better off you'll be.

As we'll further discuss later in this book, innovative ideas can come from anywhere in the corporation. The cross-functional participation of a balanced team can help the innovator—whoever they may be—learn from the process of developing the business as well as making the innovation bulletproof. By considering the various angles across business functions, you can ensure that the business plan for the innovation is robust enough to stand up to scrutiny and challenge from higher-level executives.

Of pigs, chickens, and commitment

"Why can't we just call up our legal/finance/sales/marketing team when we need them to answer a question for us?"

We have been asked this time and time again. The answer is best told in the allegory of the chicken and the pig, often shared by Agile and Scrum development teams.

> *A pig and a chicken are walking around the farm together when the chicken stops and says, "Hey Pig, I have a great idea. Let's open a breakfast restaurant together." The pig thinks about it a moment and says, "Sure, why not? But what shall we call it?" The chicken, being the brains of the operation, says, "I know! We can call it Ham & Eggs!" The pig thinks about it and replies, "If we go that direction, I'll be fully committed and you will just be involved."*

Now is the answer clear? It all comes down to involvement versus commitment. When you call upon the resources of the various teams in your company, you get their involvement in the project. No doubt they are seriously involved: aiming to deliver valuable conversation and guidance. But without being fully committed to your success, are they merely consultants giving out the best advice they can muster at that moment?

Are they just chickens?

What innovation needs is full commitment with gusto and passion...and without hesitation. Form a diverse innovation team explicitly with experts who are 110 percent fully committed to the success of the innovation at hand. Tap special people to join this innovation team because, in the end, what you want is a team that is fully committed.

You want a team of pigs.

You want a commitment that extends beyond advice and guidance and enters the realm of ownership. Through deep and rich involvement in the innovation process, these accountants, lawyers, and marketers become something greater. They become champions for each and every worthy innovation that comes through the door. The difference between the chicken and the pig in innovation development is the difference between simply giving advice and shepherding a fledgling idea along.

The secret to nurturing a fully committed team is providing them with something that they can continuously be fully committed to, day in and day out. One of the biggest challenges, as you have read in the prior pages, is ensuring that the innovation team has a continuous flow of brilliant ideas to back up. Nothing can bolster the commitment of an innovation team more than providing them something for which they can stand up and fight. Genuinely committed team members who believe in the process and the outputs will harness all of their technical prowess and political capital in their areas of expertise to help a new and worthy innovation gain the traction it needs to grow and develop.

How do you create full commitment? Create full engagement from the beginning of the process—when an idea bubbles up to the surface for initial review. The conversations, the idea exchanges, the intellectual jousting over the value and prospects that take place in those initial reviews create enormous amounts of energy. The excitement and optimism about the potential of the ideas being reviewed is what will get your team fully engaged in every great idea.

The biggest challenge, then, is in finding a way to keep that positive energy flowing, day in and day out.

Personalities of Innovation

Unlike work functions, work personalities create value in those moments when a team is not counting, drawing, or selling. It is the experimenting, collaborating, connecting, and sharing that's not explicitly part of the job description. The way you work, the way you approach challenges, the actions you take intuitively are all part of your work personality.

It could be argued that work personalities are more important to embrace than work functions. We're not talking about the Myers-Briggs, DISC, or some other personality test you had to suffer through at your corporate office job. Those test how you are operating in your work function. We are more interested in the moments in between your work. It's something more ethereal and interesting. It's the moments spent creating connections, transferring ideas, daydreaming, stargazing, problem solving, aspiring, and everything else we do that generates immeasurable value.

In 2005, Tom Kelley and Jonathan Littman penned a thought-provoking book called *The Ten Faces of Innovation* based on their work at IDEO, a consumer products innovation laboratory. Regarding how the IDEO team approached innovation, Kelley and Littman said:

> *"At IDEO, we've developed 10 people-centric tools, talents or personas for innovation. Although the list does not presume to be comprehensive, it does aspire to expand your repertoire. We've found that adopting one or more of these roles can help teams express a different point of view and create a broader range of innovative solutions."*[2]

Kelley and his IDEO team used these personalities and personas while addressing new ideas and developing solutions. It helped because it forced

---

2 Tom Kelley and Jonathan Littman, "The 10 Faces of Innovation," *Fast Company*, October 2005, http://www.fastcompany.com/54102/10-faces-innovation.

naturally creative people to take on roles and perspectives that were foreign to them in order to force a change in point of view. The technique was a powerful way to expand thinking and enhance the level and depth of consideration given to a problem or challenge. While not necessarily asking lawyers to think like designers or accountants to think like marketers, the practice asked participants to think outside of their own "boxes."

Encouraging your team members to "try on" personas is certainly valuable. There is even greater value in seeking out team members with inherent personalities. In other words, it is one thing to ask a person to take on a persona or a point of view in order to force a new perspective; it is entirely different when you are actively choosing that person for their persona and natural point of view. It is always much more natural to assert/ defend your perspective when it is your own, as opposed to a perspective you are asked to assume.

So what are the kinds of personalities that are best suited to internal innovation efforts? You may be surprised to learn larger-than-life innovation rock stars are not necessarily among them. While other organizations aspire to have that one Steve Jobs or Thomas Edison within their ranks, be on the lookout for personalities who know how to get the work done. The challenges you will face when creating an innovation center and then delivering on your promise of new product development will not be conquerable by one person—or personality—alone. You are going to require the resourcefulness, creativity, and cunning of a cast of characters.

Personalities Within Your Innovation Team

Common descriptions of the personalities required for innovation are suggestive and demonstrative. In every company in every corner of the globe, creative and driven employees are figuring out ways to get things done within—or in spite of—their corporate culture. Here we offer some of the more common traits and encourage you to add your own. We would be especially appreciative if you shared your additions to this list with us.

One word of caution while you read on: Personalities do not dictate roles.

Personality is the way an individual approaches the task at hand. While it would seem natural to assign a Conductor to always be a project manager and an Alchemist to be involved with R&D, resist the urge. Allow your team to engage with each of the innovation projects in ways that are meaningful and valuable to them. Their personalities should complement their work and the work being done by the other members of the team. Period.

The Conductor

Think of a Conductor and a few common images likely pop into your mind: someone who is leading an orchestra or someone who is managing a train. In either case, you're right. In terms of an internal innovation enterprise, the Conductor is the individual who sets the strategic vision of the team and steers them through the entire experience. Why is this a personality and not a skill set? In some rare cases, the managing director may not necessarily be the Conductor.

The nuance of the Conductor personality lies in how the individual is able to extract the best out of all of the other personalities and to create a smooth-running operation. Like a musical Conductor, this individual needs to know when to enlist the voices of each stakeholder group, and when to dampen the others. He or she manages the volume, the tempo, and (ultimately) the public perception of the group. The Conductor must be able to move and align the team members ad hoc to achieve the best blend of talent—at the right moment—on each project.

Are you picturing a traditional organizational leader? You may be missing the point. While the Conductor is a natural leader, this person need not be the face of the operation. You are looking for a goal-oriented expert in managing people. In effect, someone who can help the team self-organize in a way that it runs effectively and in perfect harmony. This may not be done by directing the agenda and conversations but with subtle nudges and suggestions.

Extraordinary Conductors we've worked with have had the uncanny ability to use subtlety to create an exceptional outcome. While they may have large leadership personalities, Conductors know when and how to wield their influence to great effect.

The Cat Burglar

While it may not be politically correct to assume (or even admit) that you have a Cat Burglar personality in your organization, the truth is that you do. Trust us. You do. And whether or not you are aware of their presence, they exist. They're lurking in your break rooms, casing your business, and learning your organizational vulnerabilities.

The reality is that Cat Burglars are almost always benign and their personalities stem mostly from institutional frustration. They often spend their time ferreting out organizational loopholes, side doors, and workarounds because they struggled to get their initiatives put through and were forced to find an easier way. We call them Cat Burglars because they have an innate ability to move through and around organizational messes undetected and to come out the other end with their goals met and prizes seized.

Use Cat Burglars to your advantage. They often know all of the tricks and hacks that can help accomplish what stumps other people. For instance, a Cat Burglar once shared a tip with our co-author Randal regarding expense reporting while he served as an innovation leader at a previous job. She taught him that how expense reports (GL codes, cost centers, and values) were filled out on projects determined whether or not they were flagged for review. Since a flagged report required extra paperwork, he and his team developed a system based on her insight. Same dollar values, same payers, same receipts. But different entry formats and much less time spent doing non-value-added work.

In another instance, Randal faced a budgeting protocol issue with a funded innovator. A Cat Burglar was quick with a work-around solution. She never accepted "no" for an answer and, due to her persistent pushing and skirting of the rules, she helped at least three innovations make it all the way through the development round.

The best part about Cat Burglars is that they challenge convention. They are always thinking and looking for a vulnerability or an angle to take. Cat Burglars are not malicious or contrarian. They just don't accept rules as given and look for easier and more efficient ways to get things done. They can help new innovators move in and around organizational systems with ease and intellectually challenge their assumptions. They can be some of the most fun and resourceful people you employ.

The Reverse Engineer

The Reverse Engineer is a wonderfully curious personality. Never one to take anything at face value, the Reverse Engineer is constantly thinking and asking questions like, "I wonder if we can do that here?" and, "How exactly does that widget do its job?" The Reverse Engineer need not be an actual engineer. Rather, they are simply the one with an unmistakable and burning desire to understand things at a level that is one, two, or even three levels deeper than anyone else on the team cares to dig.

Since Reverse Engineers are obsessed with understanding how things work, they can be the most valuable members of your team for many reasons. First of all, the Reverse Engineer will be the individual who challenges the assumptions of your ideators. They will pursue lines of questioning all the way back to the most granular level. They are never satisfied until they can comprehend not only what the proposal does but how it does it, fully testing the assumptions the system's success are built on. A Reverse Engineer leaves no stone unturned and no widget un-widgeted.

The Reverse Engineer, through a unique thought process, has the ability to look outside the organization, deconstruct amazing things, and find ways to integrate them into your organization. For better or worse, Reverse Engineers are often let down the most often. They have a passion for doing things better, systematically speaking, and striving to bring new best practices into the organization. Oftentimes, to their chagrin, they find that there are not enough resources or organizational will to undertake the latest and greatest innovation that they know can be integrated into the organization immediately. But here's what you can do: Channel that frustration into passion for your innovation projects.

Funded innovators usually react the same way to Reverse Engineers: They love and hate them, all at the same time. In almost every case we've witnessed, though, Reverse Engineers have given the innovator a new perspective and uncovered a potential improvement. That is exactly why you want them on your innovation team.

The Ambassador

The Ambassador is the glad-handing, chatty extrovert who takes great pains to welcome and connect newcomers. Genial, genuine, and always willing to offer a hand, the Ambassador is the kind of personality that you want as the public-facing representative of your innovation effort. These personalities come from every skill set in your organization. It's generally a great idea to have a few Ambassadors because they are fantastic at working with new innovators.

Ambassadors, by nature, are extroverts and supportive individuals. Their role is to provide exceptional liaisons between individual innovators and the innovation team. In most cases, Ambassadors are highly connected people within the organization—if only because they make it their business to be well-connected to everyone else. More often than not, their connected networks are based on social conversations and points of connection. This is important because, when it comes time to asking for favors, having a well-connected Ambassador can be the difference between success and failure. It is the Ambassador's uncanny ability to build a network and strategically leverage the value within it that makes this individual such a valuable personality within your innovation team.

Would you believe that most executive assistants are natural Ambassadors? In fact, they have been some of the strongest Ambassador personalities we've ever seen on innovation teams. Just think about it: Great EAs have robust personal networks across every department in the organization. They can connect funded innovators with key players with just a phone call. So, when you are assembling your team, don't overlook potential members simply because of their job titles.

The Alchemist

Every organization has a group of Alchemists who, in their spare time, are looking for ways to cook up new and interesting concoctions. They're mad scientists, if you will. The Alchemist has an insatiable urge to experiment and try new things in one-off experiments or in combination with other existing programs. Alchemists learn through doing. Often, this takes the shape of rough-cut prototypes-as-side projects.

The creative genius that is the Alchemist has the hubris to attempt and envision the end state of overly ambitious experimentations. And, quite honestly, they aren't concerned whether or not the experiments are destined to fail. The Alchemist is the eternal optimist, which makes the personality a perfect complement to any innovation team.

Since the Alchemist has little fear of failure, it is this individual who will push the innovation team to test the bounds of conventional wisdom.

But, contrary to what you may be thinking, it's the Alchemist who brings a lot of credibility to the table. Why? They have tried and failed throughout their careers. Consequently, they bring plenty of perfect 20/20 hindsight. Their successes and failures have taught them many valuable lessons, lessons they are eager to share with novice innovators who are just getting their first taste of what it is like to innovate.

A warning about Alchemists: When you pair them with innovators, make sure that they understand their role both in terms of their specific skill set and their personality. An Alchemist left unchecked can distract and derail an innovator by continually suggesting additions and augmentations. It's their nature. Don't fight them. Manage them.

The Robin Hood

Robin Hood, the eponymous character of old English lore, stole from the rich and gave to the poor. So, wait, are we hinting at corporate espionage? Hardly. In our personality profile, Robin Hood deals in the currency of ideas: bringing back old ideas and uncovering new ones through keen observation and engagement.

Robin Hood personalities are always on the lookout for new ideas, technology, and the next big thing. They have a penchant for looking outside of the organization and even outside the field to find genuinely new and interesting ideas, bringing them back to the innovation team for consideration. For better or for worse, they are subject to "shiny things syndrome" and can easily be distracted with the latest iteration of technology or next big thing.

Robin Hood personalities are exceptional at bringing in new, interesting ideas. When partnering with innovators in the development process, they can bring invaluable external insight and expansion ideas. They can also serve as a gut check, telling innovators when they've seen similar solutions or ideas out in the market, and then connect them to a service provider or solution that could save the innovator time and money.

Everyone has a little Robin Hood in them. Bringing that out in every employee in your organization is a key to your overall success. Keep your Robin Hood motivated and engaged by challenging that person to predict trends based on the new ideas and tools they are seeing in the marketplace. It is another way to multiply their value.

The Astronomer

While Robin Hood is out looking for ideas and solutions, the Astronomer is looking outward in search of problems to solve. It may seem odd to be actively looking for problems but, in a sense, that is an effective way for organizations to identify new growth markets.

Astronomers typically have robust institutional knowledge and understand the limitations and capabilities of their organizations. They often propose challenges that are solvable with existing resources or they know the additional resources that would be needed to solve the problems they are bringing forth.

Astronomers are valuable to innovation teams because they round out the innovation effort. While the team is out formally soliciting ideas from the greater community (which we'll cover later in the book), the Astronomer is seeking out problems to solve. We have seen numerous companies take the approach of issuing innovation challenges in which they present a problem to the company and call for ideas on how to solve the problem. It is more directed innovation work and, because it is more directed, it can produce more relevant new business lines and products.

The challenge with Astronomers is that they can overwhelm your innovation team with problems to solve. The sky is so vast and opportunities so great that without focus you will never find anything of worth. But the good news is that an Astronomer can be refocused to identify really relevant problems to use in innovation challenges.

The Navigator

The Navigator holds the maps to all of the places you may go. They know the territory, the routes, the pitfalls, and the roadblocks. In most cases, the Navigator has been down this route before and has the battle scars to prove it. More than just knowing where to go, they know where *not* to go and can make sure you stay off of that path.

The Navigator personality tends to be involved in project management activities and has a fairly good understanding of how internal processes work. They thrive on figuring out how the cogs of the wheels fit together and following workflow paths to the end. They view these organizational mazes as challenges worth solving.

It may go without saying why these personalities are critical to your innovation effort. You need someone, regardless of their skill set, who has a passion and interest in helping new innovators navigate their way through the often stifling bureaucracy of your organization. Unlike the Cat Burglar who is always in search of alternate workarounds, Navigators tend to work through the systems and can provide exceptional guidance. They work very well when partnered with the right Ambassadors.

The most successful Navigators can come from project-centric roles. They have strong experiences in working through corporate IT, finance, and project management minefields. For instance, Navigators can be supremely adept at helping innovators craft ideas and proposals that do not require such things as IT charters or PMO reviews. Oftentimes, the only person who knows how to craft and word proposals in that way are people on the inside of those functions. In other words, it's good to have an insider on your team.

The Librarian

Think about all of the ideas that came before you. Consider all of the trials and successes and failures that preceded you. Now, imagine what you and your team could have learned if only you had the documents and stories from those events. That is why you need a Librarian.

The Librarian is interested in telling the story of your work, as well as bringing to light the stories of work past. Part troubadour, part documentarian, part historian, the Librarian helps the team position its work and the innovators position their creations. They are the recorders and keepers of all history. Librarians tend to be well-seasoned, long-serving employees who have seen ideas come and go. Use them as the point of reference when familiar ideas come in, to provide deep insight into the history of why they succeeded or failed.

The Librarian reminds personalities such as the Astronomer, Alchemist, and Robin Hood of past ventures. Together they create a critical-thinking mass that can address new potential innovations or problems to solve with forward thinking and critical hindsight. Librarians are critical personas because, as we all know, history often repeats itself.

At the American Cancer Society, our Librarian was a 30-year veteran when we asked him to join the innovation team. He had so much institutional knowledge that he could recount stories of failed projects from 1980s and 1990s so that we could steer our innovator away from those paths. In the end, his allegories and anecdotes saved us hundreds of thousands of dollars by preventing us from repeating the mistakes of the past.

The Scout

The Scout is the utility player of the group, armed with some organizational knowledge, some intellectual curiosity, and some leadership ability. In a sense, the Scout knows a little about everything. While not as passionate about any one area, they are typically strong counterparts to innovators who need some guidance and coaching, but not too much. They excel as a general sounding board for new innovators and as a first point of contact.

One strategic choice that has worked in the past is to graduate funded innovators to serve as Scouts for new innovators. In almost every case, these previously funded innovators had Scout personalities. Innovators are utility players at heart and mind which make them, regardless of their formal skill sets, outstanding supporting players to other innovators.

Diversity Is Critical

The goal here is to produce an innovation team—or IGNITE team, if you're working within the IGNITE Framework—that is exceptionally diverse: Diverse in their work history, diverse in their innovation personalities, and diverse in their perspectives. Ray Mabus, Secretary of the United States Navy, spoke very candidly to NPR about the importance of team diversity and its impact on innovation.

"A more diverse force is a stronger force," he stated. "A more diverse mindset makes you a stronger force. If you have the same outlook, and the same mindset, you don't get more innovation."[3]

---

3 *All Things Considered* (Radio Interview), "Navy Secretary Believes Combat Positions Should Be Open to Qualified Women," *NPR*, September 11, 2015, http://www.npr.org/player/v2/mediaPlayer.html?action=1&t=1&islist= false&id=439381272&m=439381273&live=1.

Chapter 6: Crowdsourcing, Co-creation, and Crowdshaping

When we talk to executives about the IGNITE Framework of innovation within their businesses or nonprofits, we often talk about the need to get as many people involved in initial ideation as possible. These are the ideas that will be vetted by the innovation team. Part of the challenge in doing this for your own organization is in developing an easy and productive—yet meaningful—way to engage your community in the process. The success of implementing the IGNITE Framework, or any other innovation system, hinges in part on an ability to create a culture of engagement within the organization. As we've stated in other chapters, bad culture equals no engagement and no ideas.

Tools to achieve group ideation have evolved in recent years. More people are pooling personal data, consumer and donor profiles, and individual preferences to shape new ideas, products, and services. Whether consciously or unconsciously, intentionally or unintentionally, we're sharing this information every single day. It is fast becoming an inherent and expected part of everyday life. These ideas of group thinking and group work have gained acceptance through the use of what we call crowdsourcing and co-creation. And, more recently, we've seen the rise of a new term: crowdshaping.

Before we go any further, let's define these terms and touch on how you may decide to use them to initiate group ideation.

Crowdsourcing

The term crowdsourcing is only about 10 years old. It's usually attributed to Jeff Howe and Mark Robinson of *Wired*, who together coined the term in 2005 after conversations about how businesses were using the Internet to outsource work to individuals.[1]

While the term was just recently introduced to our lexicon, the concept is a century old. Even in the absence of online technology, the idea was hatched and has persisted to this day. A 1907 issue of *Nature* mentions: "At a 1906 country fair in Plymouth, eight hundred people participated in a contest to estimate the weight of a slaughtered and dressed ox. Statistician Francis Galton observed that the median guess, 1,207 pounds, was accurate within 1 percent of the true weight of 1,198 pounds."[2]

Howe explains that "crowdsourcing represents the act of a company or institution taking a function once performed by employees and outsourcing it to an undefined (and generally large) network of people in the form of an open call. This can take the form of peer-production (when the job is performed collaboratively), but is also often undertaken by sole individuals. The crucial prerequisite is the use of the open call format and the large network of potential laborers."[3]

1 "Crowdsourcing," *Wikipedia*, accessed December 5, 2015, http://en.wikipedia.org/wiki/crowdsourcing.
2 Francis Galton, "Vox populi," *Nature*, volume 75 (1907), pp. 450–45.
3 Jeff Howe, "Crowdsourcing: A Definition," *Macroblog entry for Crowdsourcing: Why the Power of the Crowd Is Driving the Future of Business*, June 2, 2006, http://crowdsourcing.typepad.com/cs/2006/06/crowdsourcing_a.html.

As we think about the open call for innovation, the last sentence in Howe's description is key. The IGNITE Framework addresses both crowdsourcing and the next term we'll discuss in this chapter: co-creation. These tactics differ in semantics but, more importantly, they differ in terms of active versus passive participation and scale.

Crowdsourcing usually consists of a substantially large participant pool and relatively low commitment. Participants often are superficially engaged via offering up opinions, participating in surveys, or even simply having their data used for research and decision making. Today, thanks to easy access to user and customer data, crowdsourcing has evolved to the point that it can be done with little effort on the part of the participants.

Think of the programs and services intelligently reshaped by the aggregated data on the preferences or behavior of large numbers of consumers. Consumers get a more functional, efficient service shaped not by opinions of the crowd, but around the way people truly behave. And— unlike with many existing crowdsourced solutions—they get it effortlessly, via a passive sharing of data.

That's what IBM promised when it made bus route improvements in Africa. During May 2013, the IBM Dublin Research Laboratory used cell phone data to aid the re-design of bus routes across Abidjan, the Ivory Coast's largest city. Researchers used time and location data—collected from calls and SMS—to assess commuters' frequent routes and then compared these to the existing public transport infrastructure. According to the data, there were 65 possible improvements that could reduce travel time by 10 percent.[4] This data was provided by commuters with no effort on their part.

---

4 Steve Hamm, "Insights in Motion: Deep Analytics Show How Cities Really Work," *Building a Smarter Planet: A Smarter Planet Blog*, January 17, 2013, http://asmarterplanet.com/blog/2013/01/two-cities-in-motion-a-view-into-the-life-of-a-place.html.

Co-creation

Co-creation occurs when a company goes beyond merely listening to customers and employees and starts to create with them. Instead of a select group of internal management making "yes" or "no" decisions on programs and products, it's instead opened up for discussion among a larger employee or customer base. Effectively, we look at co-creation as active collaboration with stakeholders. It differs from crowdsourcing in that the participating audience is more narrowly defined as employees, customers, and potentially key stakeholders including vendors, business partners, and hired agents.

Scholars C.K. Prahalad and Venkat Ramaswamy popularized the concept in their early-2000 *Harvard Business Review* article, "Co-Opting Customer Competence."[5] According to the authors, the true value of a product, service, or program will be increasingly co-created by the business and the customer together, instead of being created entirely by management or inside the business.

In their view, co-creation describes a trend of jointly creating products. But it also describes a movement away from customers buying products and services as transactions, to customers participating as part of a larger experience.

For a great example of co-creation, you need look no further than your friendly neighborhood Starbucks Coffee Company. Every few months, it seems, the coffee king announces some figuratively (and, often, literally) buzzworthy news. In-app ordering. Coffee delivery. A coffee on your birthday. The introduction of the "Flat White" to U.S. markets. And, most recently, ditching artificial caramel coloring and adding real pumpkin flavoring to the beloved Pumpkin Spice Latte. What do these initiatives have in common? They all originated as ideas pitched by a loyal fan base and co-created by Starbucks.

---

5 C.K. Prahalad and Venkatram Ramaswamy, "Co-opting Customer Competence," *Harvard Business Review*, January-February 2000 issue, https://hbr.org/2000/01/co-opting-customer-competence/ar/1.

You could say Starbucks is respected as much for its community as for its coffee. Launched in 1998, Starbucks' co-creation site "My Starbucks Idea" is still running strong.[6] The site simply asks coffee fans the world over, "What's your idea?" This casual approach to co-creation reflects the attitudes and behaviors of Starbucks' core consumers. Ideas are vetted and shaped by the community with very little initial guidance or interference by Starbucks. The ideas that float to the top are further developed by the Starbucks team. By the time the idea is put into action, it already has built-in awareness and support from Starbucks' biggest fans.

By 2013, the site had garnered more than 150,000 ideas with 2 million votes cast for and against those ideas. Forums likes Starbucks' also give companies insights into topics on the minds of their core consumers— whether positive or negative. One negative topic that gained considerable attention was the rumor that Starbucks did not support U.S. military troops overseas. The topic gained thousands of "thumbs up" as people bought into the rumor.

In reality, Starbucks had an existing positive relationship with the U.S. military. Although this topic was definitely off-topic to the idea of product development, Starbucks allowed the community to vent their opinions, and used the opportunity to clarify their support of American soldiers to their loudest and most loyal critics.[7]

Crowdshaping

According to trendwatching.com's research, crowdshaping is "real-time shaping (and reshaping) of a service around the preferences of the people in an office, a restaurant, on a plane: any space *right now*."[8] By this very definition, crowdshaping works best within a small universe of collaborators, because change happens in real (or near-real) time.

---

6 Visit the "My Starbucks Idea" site at www.mystarbucksidea.com, accessed December 5, 2015.
7 "Our Best Idea Was Asking You For Yours," *My Starbucks Idea blog post*, April 24, 2013, http://blogs.starbucks.com/blogs/customer/archive/2013/04/24/our-best-idea-was-asking-you-for-yours.aspx.
8 This and subsequent references to trendwatching.com are from: *Trendingwatching.com* Trend Briefing, "7 Consumer Trends to Run With in 2014," January 2014, http://trendwatching.com/trends/7trends2014/.

A simple example of this is Rockbot: an app that allows patrons to pick the music playing at restaurants, bars, and businesses right from their phones.[9] Users register via the app, and enter their favorite songs for a set list to the music queue when they're at a venue that uses the service. Users also have the option to vote on the songs others select. Love rocking out a song from Black Moth Super Rainbow or The Octopus Project? Get your friends to up vote it. The app made its splash as Roqbot at SXSW 2011, where it won grand prize in the SXSW Accelerator® competition.[10]

The key to being exceptional at crowdshaping is agility, flexibility, and speed. Not all businesses or situations are right for crowdshaping. Others, however, have already utilized the concept in a way that has already changed your own encounters every day. Many retail stores crowdshape, opening and closing register lanes in response to customer wait times. Restaurants that frequently change their menu are crowdshaping based on consumer preferences. With the emergence of 3D printing, manufacturing may soon adopt some crowdshaping practices in order to more readily respond to consumer demands and competitive challenges.

Bridging These Tools

At the beginning of this chapter, we took the position that these practices would combine and evolve over time in response to technology and consumer preferences. In fact, as industry and consumers alike begin to fully understand the power and value of collaborative development, we are seeing technology fundamentally change our relationship with businesses. Here's how:

In today's complex consumer landscape, we all leave behind digital trails, just as IBM Dublin Research Laboratory discovered in our earlier example. In *The Filter Bubble*, Eli Pariser speaks about the future of personalization

---

9 Learn more about Rockbot at https://rockbot.com/, accessed December 5, 2015.
10 For innovation inspiration, check out this and other past SXSW Accelerator winners here: *"SXSW Accelerator Alums: Over $2.6 Billion in Funding,"* accessed December 5, 2015, http://www.sxsw.com/interactive/accelerator-alums.

within this context: "Signals about our personal behavior and the computing power necessary to crunch through them are becoming cheaper than ever to acquire."[11]

In fact, when you search on Google, it uses 57 "signals" (last time we checked, it changes all the time)—from your location to your last online purchase—to make an educated guess about who you are and what content best suits you. Companies now combine this with social media, web histories, e-commerce, endless read/listen/watch/playlists, smartphone and tablet GPS services and more. The connected consumers are creating vast profiles and data trails that relate to everything from music preferences to daily movements.

According to the folks at trendwatching.com, the future will see two certainties:

- The technologies that facilitate the creation and passive sharing of those data streams will become even more ubiquitous.

- Consumer expectations are only going to be amplified—*yet again*—by that ubiquity.

So, as the connected crowd comes of age, not only are they open to their data being utilized, they'll come to expect it. What's more, they'll expect to offer ideas based on that data through co-creation and—in some instances—expect immediate results by seeing that input (crowdsourcing) and those directly offered ideas (co-creation) turned into change (crowdshaping).

Although these uses of technology to shape our future are exciting, we want to be very clear here: Crowdsourcing, co-creation, and crowdshaping are *not* innovation, per se. They are ways to engage your community in the initial steps of the larger innovation process. To confuse these tactics with innovation itself is dangerous because they are a means to an end,

11 Eli Pariser, *The Filter Bubble: How the New Personalized Web Is Changing What We Read and How We Think*, reprint edition (London: Penguin Books, 2012).

not the end itself. In a well-managed innovation framework like IGNITE, companies use crowdsourcing, co-creation, and crowdshaping to generate and collect broad opinions and ideas and to identify problems to solve.

To spur activity, the innovation team may opt to proactively search for ideas and put forth a call for ideas around a specific problem or ideation challenge, seeking broad community input. This is where the IGNITE Framework shines.

To further explain this, imagine a large organization that has just launched a co-creation program and an online community to benefit that program. In the past, most participants wanting to engage in the internal program endured tedious manual methods to submit suggestions. Those suggestions were coming from over-worked staff who would lose the email address for the suggestion box, be forced to hand-write in triplicate, or suffer through submitting via a 1-800 number or office voicemail. All too often, suggestions sat in a long-lost pile of dusty old surveys in the basement next to Milton or Janice from accounting. Other lucky staff had the option of a spider-web covered, gum wrapper-filled suggestion box in the hallway.

As you can imagine, this process was not scalable, and provided little transparency to the individuals who submitted the original suggestions.

An online, password-protected, ideation platform combined with the process of IGNITE (as we'll discuss later), can now give that company's employees and stakeholders their own suggestion platform, transparency in ideas submitted, a true voice for new ideas, and a formalized process for being heard.

For staff and management, an online idea hub plus the IGNITE Framework provides a scalable way to co-create new ideas with stakeholders and active partners. Traditionally feedback and market research has come in the form of user groups/focus groups or one-on-one interactions with staff. These traditional approaches are still beneficial but do not scale to large audiences or support shorter implementation cycles to bring out the best new ideas for new business opportunities, services, or programs. This new approach does.

Inspiration to Get You Started

To better illustrate how crowdsourcing, co-creation, and crowdshaping can be accomplished through an online ideation platform, we've curated a few examples below. Most of these are hits, some are misses, and not all of them contain all the ingredients for success. However, they're all great places to start.

Dell IdeaStorm

Dell is one of the world's largest private providers of computer equipment and enterprise-level technology services. It was also one of the first companies to allow customers to custom-build their own computers online and have them delivered directly to their homes. This heritage of listening to the customers and dealing with them directly has a clear link to Dell's online ideation and crowdsourcing site, IdeaStorm.

From Dell.com, "IdeaStorm was created to give a direct voice to Dell customers and an avenue to have online 'brainstorm' sessions to allow you the customer to share ideas and collaborate with one another and Dell. Our goal through IdeaStorm is to hear what new products or services you'd like to see Dell develop. We hope this site fosters a candid and robust conversation about your ideas." [12]

Since the site was launched in 2007, Dell's IdeaStorm team has collected more than 23,000 ideas and implemented an estimated 550. In December 2009, Dell added "Storm Sessions" where Dell posts a specific topic and asks customers to submit ideas. In a sense, Dell is asking its engaged consumers to "guess the weight" of the ox, and they are using the most common, or average of, the responses as the best possible answer.

---

12 Learn more about IdeaStorm at http://www.ideastorm.com/idea2AboutIdeaStorm?v=1386335794051, accessed December 5, 2015.

More recently, Dell added even more sophistication to the process by allowing idea "Extensions." With an "Extension," an idea poster can promote a comment made on their original idea, enabling ideas to evolve over time through collaboration: a leap forward in enabling more intimate co-creation among their participants.

Dell has done a remarkable job in its efforts to deploy two platforms for crowdsourcing and co-creation. It has established a well-respected, well-curated space in which Dell itself can submit challenges that it wants solved (crowdsourcing) while providing a space for users to collaborate and refine their own ideas with the help of others (co-creation).

One big takeaway here is that Dell evolved the platform over time. One of the very first ideas submitted and approved back in 2007 (in fact, two days after the site launched) is the need for a moderator from Dell to curate the discussions on the platform. According to the idea submitter, "Approximately 48 hours into its life…IdeaStorm is filling up with repetition and senseless comments. Since moderation cannot be exercised by the participants a moderator a la Dell Employee must put up her hand. Or his hand. We aren't picky!"[13]

This idea received 1,151 votes. Think about it: In Dell's effort to create a transparent and completely open forum, it was the community that asked for Dell to step in and offer additional rules and guidance. Then, over time, the opportunities to add "Storm Sessions" and "Extensions" became apparent. A well-managed online ideation platform gives you the tools to learn, grow, evolve, and improve the process as needed.

The Giffgaff community

Giffgaff is a small telecommunications company in the UK. The company rents its mobile network from a larger carrier and sells pre-paid SIM cards to its customers. It also actively competes against the traditional

---

13 "The Clutter is Forming: We Need a Moderator," *IdeaStorm* post, accessed December 5, 2015, http://www.ideastorm.com/idea2ReadIdea?v=1443763997763&Id=0877000000006p5AAA.

UK telecom companies. Unlike most mobile operators, Giffgaff does not have a traditional call center. In fact, it has just a handful of employees. How does its system work? By handing control over to customers. The company utilizes crowdsourcing in its customer support and co-creation is in its product development.

According to Laurence Buchanan of the Customer Revolution blog, "Right from set-up Giffgaff engaged their target market in two-way dialogue, asking potential customers and early adopters to decide on how best to structure their tariffs."[14] When last we looked, more than 10,000 ideas had been submitted, with more than 500 implemented.[15] That's a remarkable record! A 5 percent implementation mark is extraordinary considering that most innovation systems are expected to achieve 1 to 2 percent implementation.

New idea	This is a brand new idea
Working on it	Ideas currently in development
Implemented	This idea is now a working feature of giffgaff
We're looking into it	We will need to investigate factors of this idea before making a decision
Under consideration	Ideas we like but there are obstacles in the way. It will be brought up in a prioritisation meeting and reviewed regularly
Not for us	Unfortunately this idea isn't right for us

Source: https://labs.giffgaff.com/how

---

14 Laurence Buchanan, "GiffGaff—A case study of customers in control," *The Customer Revolution blog*, December 9, 2010, http://thecustomerevolution.blogspot.com/2010/12/giffgaff-case-study-of-customers-in.html.
15 For more on Giffgaff and how it works, visit https://labs.giffgaff.com/how, accessed December 5, 2015.

While Giffgaff uses co-creation in its product development, it also handles customer service using intelligence gathered from the "wisdom of the crowds." The company pushes all service issues to its community first and also publishes FAQs and tips-and-tricks on a regular basis. This effort collects the best solutions to the technical issues experienced by consumers and publishes them for all to see.

But where we see a real difference between Giffgaff and most telecoms is in the cost savings realized by implementing a crowdsourced support system. This approach enables true peer-to-peer support and only occasionally requires support from Giffgaff employees. According to Buchanan, "The community has radically cut customer support costs compared to the traditional contact centre-centric model. They estimated that if the large telecom O2 could replicate the model with just 25 percent of their customers participating, they could save $20m Euros per year."

We see a similar trend of peer support and customer co-creation combined with the "wisdom of the crowds" across the entire landscape of customer-driven issue support. According to analysts at Forrester, customers are adopting communities for customer service at a rate that has risen from 23 percent to 32 percent. Now, an average of 42 percent of Generations X, Y, and Z adults online use communities to solve issues.[16]

These participants are your employees and consumers. Many of them (Gen Z or whatever we call it this month) are joining the workforce in the next five years. So, it's important to understand the value of online community and how it is inherent to your customers. They are primed to participate in online innovation communities that feed ideas into the IGNITE Framework.

---

16 Forrester Report by Kate Leggett with Stephen Powers, Zia Daniell Wigder, Shannon Coyne, "*Understand Communication Channel Needs To Craft Your Customer Service Strategy*," March 11, 2013, http://www.forrester.com/Understand+Communication+Channel+Needs+To+Craft+Your+Customer+Service+Strategy/fulltext/-/E-RES88421?isTurnHighlighting=false&highlightTerm=understand%20communication%20channel%20needs.

Lenovo Superfans

Lenovo is a large computer electronics brand that is mostly known for making laptops. When IBM sold its laptop business to Lenovo in 2004, the lesser-known company experienced a major shift: The acquisition required them to transform from a traditional corporate (B2B) sales organization into a consumer-facing (B2C) company. A big part of this shift was Lenovo's move to support its changing business model through crowdsourcing.

These days, Lenovo is known for involving its community in resolving technical support issues, similar to Giffgaff. The community runs with a moderation team composed of customer volunteers from all over the world.

Part of the success Lenovo is experiencing comes from its willingness to turn over control of its community and solutions for development to its most loyal and knowledgeable fans. That's crowd ideation at its best. Lenovo actively sought out early adopters and persistent users for consideration as "superfans." Over a period of three years, approximately 30 superfans contributed 1,200 knowledge base articles and 44 percent of accepted technical issue solutions.[17]

Lenovo tapped into these superfans before the formal community even launched. The Lenovo community manager listened to these superfans and enlisted their help in the community's initial design, policies, rules, and content. Here's how the community contributed:

- One member revised the contributor rank and reward structure to make it more flexible and to recognize diverse ways of contributing.

- One member designed all the graphics for the leader pages.

- One member introduced a new skin (graphic design) and tabbed navigation style for the different engagement styles within the community.

---

17 For more about Lenovo's superfans, see http://www.lithium.com/customer-stories/lenovo, accessed December 6, 2015.

- One member helped launch a German community by helping to localize terminology and functioning as the liaison or goodwill ambassador with the existing German forums.

Lenovo has even funded training on Lithium's Studio (the software that runs the community) and development tools for some of its superfan volunteers.

Much like you might focus your community on ideation or specific ideation challenges, Lenovo focuses its energy on encouraging its community to contribute a certain number of support articles. Once a certain threshold of activity and content was reached, focus moved toward curation, or turning answers into knowledge base articles. The folks at Lenovo soon surpassed their initial goal of 500 articles, receiving more than 1,200 articles as of 2013. In fact, the original internal company policy was to vet all articles after the initial 500, but the management team soon realized the contributors were experts, and so they decided to stop reviewing the articles and allow the superfans to self-monitor the content being posted.

In dollar terms, Lenovo is realizing huge cost savings by doing this. The company estimated that it would have cost thousands of dollars to produce each one of the knowledge base articles, given the topic complexity and the expertise of people involved. For its internal ROI metrics, Lenovo estimated that—at a conservative $1,000 per article—it saved more than $1 million.[18]

The City of Austin crowdsourcing #FAIL

In 2010 and 2011, the City of Austin, Texas, decided to tap the community to help rename its current Solid Waste Services (SWS) department. "Our mission has changed, and with that changed mission, we need to present a different message to the public," said SWS Director Bob Gedert, reported by the *Austin Chronicle* in 2011. "Our department name can

---

18 "Lithys 2011: Digital Customer Excellence Awards," http://lithosphere.lithium.com/t5/Lithys-Social-Customer/Lithys-2011-Best-Community-Story-or-Anecdote-Lenovo/idi-p/25036.

present a new image."[19]

However, the one name picked by the crowds was likely not Gedert's top choice. More than 30,000 people voted for an entry by Austinite Kyle Hentges that called for the Solid Waste Department to be renamed "Fred Durst Society of the Humanities and Arts." News of the somewhat good-natured ribbing reached Fred Durst, the lead singer of an often-mocked band from the 90's (Limp Bizkit), who was flattered and had this to say on Twitter, "I want to thank all of you who are helping me in Austin. I hope we win."

Did the City of Austin honor the people's choice? Alas, it did not. The department was renamed "Austin Resource Recovery" in an executive overruling.

Fails like this WILL happen in your community. That's okay. How you choose to deal with them is where you can get into trouble. The City of Austin chose to let it play out.

"We knew that with Austin, we would get lots of creative input," Jennifer Herber, public information officer with Austin Resource Recovery, said. She goes on to say that the city "could've taken it down" once it became apparent the website's untenable suggestions would get the most votes but that the "point was to get public input" plus "a lot of attention." They succeeded on both fronts. In the end, the City of Austin received even more attention than they could have hoped for, from large nationwide media outlets including MTV, NPR, and more.

BMW Co-Creation Lab

BMW, a large auto manufacturer that owns the Mini Cooper and Rolls-Royce brands, launched its co-creation lab to much fanfare a few years ago. The stated goal of its online co-creation lab is "to provide a virtual meeting place for individuals interested in cars and all related topics, who

---

19 Wells Dunbar, "City Hall Hustle: Solid Waste Rocks!," *Austin Chronicle*, February 11, 2011, http://www.austinchronicle.com/news/2011-02-11/city-hall-hustle-solid-waste-rocks/.

want to collaborate with the BMW AG team in a variety of innovation-related projects and initiatives."

Now that's a straightforward mission statement that jives well with our IGNITE Framework. Here's how BMW runs its co-creation community: Customers help develop new ideas and work on concepts or solutions to the "evaluation, testing and enrichment" of existing ideas. After a comprehensive registration process—which includes questions about the types of cars you own, household income, and creating a BMW-specific username and password—applicants are then invited to participate in selected customer co-creation processes.

Although the vetting process is lengthy and rather dry (think online exam), BMW is taking a smart step in curating its co-creation community. BMW took a proactive move and chose to screen its participants. They were seeking out subject matter experts with experience in building products, applying for patents, and their reasoning behind wanting to join the community in the first place. Phrasing these questions appropriately is important, as they can easily enter the territory of being intrusive. However, there can be good value behind drawing this out of community members from the beginning.

Another point of interest with the BMW co-creation program is illustrated in its legal wording. Taken directly from their terms and services page, the site states:

> "The ideas of the Co-Creation Lab will be reviewed by internal experts of the BMW AG in order to evaluate and analyze trends, ideas, and needs concerning the respective project. Where applicable ideas of the Co-Creation Lab will be presented to persons outside of the BMW AG in an anonymous form, for example at forums for discussion. Information about the participant and his / her opinion will not be revealed."[20]

---

20 For more on the BMW Co-Creation Lab, see https://www.bmwgroup-cocreationlab.com/terms, accessed October 14, 2014.

Although we don't delve into the legal aspect of an open innovation program, this is a simple one. Be sure that all the ideas you have participants submit are covered under some sort of legal agreement. In this case BMW has a pretty liberal policy in place: only asking that they are able to talk about the ideas submitted in thought leadership activities. Other policies are a bit stricter, requiring the submitter to give up all legal rights to the idea once it's submitted! Hopefully your ideation program will fall somewhere in the middle of these two extremes.

SAP Idea Place

SAP is a German software corporation that makes enterprise software to manage business operations and customer relationships. In 2013, the company re-launched its online community network, Idea Place, with new capabilities including greater transparency for users, voting and gamification, and support for mobile.[21] Idea Place is where SAP customers can openly share their ideas with SAP for product enhancements, receive feedback from product management, and enable SAP to execute on ideas.

At the time of the relaunch, SAP Idea Place surpassed a total of 600 crowd-generated ideas implemented or in development for imminent release within SAP products. We include this SAP example to illustrate a clear need for innovation/ideation to have a home. Whether that home is an internal department or a website where users can submit and express ideas, a solid foundation is needed for any ideation program to grow.

As a software company, SAP has several avenues for evolving its products: inside meetings, user submitted feedback, bug reports both inside and outside the company, and SAP Idea Place. In fact, the number of possibilities is quite surprising, when you compare it to a product or service that's more customer-facing.

---

21 Mark Yolton, "Co-Innovating the Future with #SAP Idea Place," *SAP Community Network* blog, March 15, 2013, http://scn.sap.com/community/about/blog/2013/03/15/co-innovating-the-future-with-sap-idea-place.

Since relaunching, SAP Idea Place has realized the following:

- 8,700+ submitted ideas
- 9,000+ comments
- 53,000+ votes
- 380+ delivered features
- 260+ ideas in development & testing

Software to Help Make It Happen

There are dozens of software companies that can help with crowdsourcing, co-creation, and even crowdshaping. In the spirit of remaining objective, we've listed five leading providers of innovation software below. The list represents just a few possible ways to get started with online ideation.

Salesforce Ideas

With this ideation tool from one of the leading cloud-based CRM systems in the world, Salesforce has made its cake and is eating it, too. Salesforce uses its own platform to power IdeaExchange, its community-driven innovation hub where community members can suggest and vote on product enhancements.[22] The company defines its Ideas tool as a community of users who post, vote for, and comment on ideas; adding that the Ideas community provides an online, transparent way to attract, manage, and showcase innovation.

Salesforce boasts that the 2016 release of Ideas is the best yet and offers tips on how organizations can implement it any number of ways through the Salesforce platform: through its Customer Portal, the Salesforce

---

22 Kristie Garafola, "It's a New IdeaExchange Record! 1 Million Points Delivered Since Dreamforce '14," *Salesforce* blog, August 19, 2015, https://www.salesforce.com/blog/2015/08/ideaexchange-one-million-points.html.

console, and even its Chatter social media zone.[23] You can learn more about Ideas at Salesforce.com.

Brightidea

The folks at Brightidea claim to have launched the first-ever online innovation platform in 2005. Their online platform is designed to improve the scalability and effectiveness of any organization's innovation process. Unlike many companies in this list, Brightidea has a complete product offering called Innovation Suite that covers the entire idea lifecycle, from initial collection through execution.

The platform helped Brightidea become a Forrester Wave Innovation Leader in 2013[24] and earn high-profile clients from Bobcat to GE to United Airlines.[25] Since then, the platform has added apps to help set up, track, and compare initiatives.[26] Learn more about the platform at Brightidea.com.

For a deeper look, do us a favor: Take out your smart phone and load up your QR code app. Now, click on the QR code below to watch a great video about the HP Innovation Program as powered by the folks at Brightidea.[27]

---

23 Salesforce, "Salesforce Ideas Implementation Guide: Winter '16," October 16, 2015, http://resources.docs. salesforce.com/198/0/en-us/sfdc/pdf/salesforce_ideas_implementation_guide.pdf.
24 Chip Gliedman with Peter Burris and Nancy Wang, "The Forrester Wave™: *Innovation Management Tools, Q3 2013*," Forrester report, July 11, 2013, https://www.forrester.com/The+Forrester+Wave+Innovation+Manag ement+Tools+Q3+2013/fulltext/-/E-RES97221.
25 See http://www.brightidea.com/customers/, accessed November 28, 2015.
26 According to http://www.brightidea.com/product/, accessed November 28, 2015.
27 Don't have a code reader? Visit http://vimeo.com/39853701#, accessed December 20, 2015.

Sprinklr's GetSatisfaction

This platform is mainly used for customer feedback as opposed to ideation. But it has had some big wins in this area. TechSmith, maker of the popular software screen capture tool SnagIt, used their platform in 2011 to complete a 10-month "innovation" process with its users as they attempted to launch a Mac version. More than 120,000 topics were posted on the GetSatisfaction-powered site. These topics engaged over 450,000 people in the process as they created the new product.[28] They were acquired in 2015 by the social media management technology company Sprinklr. It will be interesting to see how they integrate this community ideation platform into their overall strategy.

HYVE Innovation Community

HYVE IdeaNet® is powerful software that not only collects crowdsourced ideas and feedback, it also functions as an internal idea and innovation-management tool, company suggestion system, and

---

28 "TechSmith Saves $500,000 by Crowdsourcing Snagit on Mac Development Research in Custom Get Satisfaction Community," TechSmith press room, April 1, 2011, http://www.techsmith.com/press-get-satisfaction-1011.html.

other idea-finding tools. HYVE is seemingly unique in that it also offers an ideation tool aimed at making government agencies more transparent. It's called Open Government. You can learn more at HYVEcommunity.net.[29]

NetworkStorms

This software platform, built by Austin, Texas, native Edward Cruz, is a smaller-scale version of the software platforms above and is a perfect choice for small business or organizations. It's a social networking platform that lets you tap into the collaborative potential of your online friends, followers, and colleagues. On NetworkStorms, you pose the questions, and your social network helps you generate ideas, solve problems, and create new opportunities. Learn more at NetworkStorms.com[30]

The platform is part of The Storms Network family, which includes PeopleStorm and GuruStorm. PeopleStorm allows organizations to engage a large, diverse online crowd. Often users will provide great answers to questions in just 24 hours. GuruStorm is a site that provides a curated crowd of business experts to help organizations solve complex, difficult problems.

Putting It into Perspective

Now that you understand the difference between crowdsourcing, co-creation, and crowdshaping, and how they can be put to use in an online ideation platform, we hope you also understand the delicate linkages these tools have between one another in the IGNITE Framework.

Consider using these examples to help you decide on the best method to implement the IGNITE Framework in your organization when it comes to generating ideas. As we will discuss in the coming chapters, the success

---

29 See https://www.hyvecommunity.net/, accessed December 6, 2015.
30 See https://www.networkstorms.com/brainstorm/welcome, accessed February 18, 2016.

of your innovation program lies in your ability to collect vast amounts of ideas and find the most valuable ones for development. Build your IGNITE Framework, establish your processes, and then activate your crowdsourcing, co-creation, and crowdshaping programs to bring in the new ideas. Let's get started.

THE IGNITE FRAMEWORK

Chapter 7: Organizing to IGNITE

In one of his earliest books, author Seth Godin speaks about factory versus farm workers. He explains that, for the first 100 years in the United States, those who made the most money were the people who had the biggest, highest-yielding farms. As the years passed and the economy shifted during the Industrial Revolution, the locus of wealth creation shifted. In the second century of U.S. history, the focus was all about who could have the biggest, highest-yielding factories. Factories and farms were "the American way" because the wealth creation paradigm in the U.S. was based on a centralized effort. The focus was on a single, large unit that created wealth through scale and concentration. Hence: big farms and big factories.

This is no longer the case in our modern economy. Single, monolithic entities are not able to generate the same scale of wealth they once did. Granted, some are doing just fine, but a number of factors have contributed to the erosion of their capacity. It's due mainly to global competition and the low cost of distributed resources. Cheap labor costs in a variety of countries from China, to Burma, to Bangladesh have forced many American factories to close, or to physically move or outsource operations overseas in order to compete.

The economic pressures are not just impacting manufacturing. Commercial farms have gradually evolved in one of two ways. There are small, locally owned farm-to-table outfits (Springdale Farms in Austin, Texas, for instance). And on the other end of the scale, there are factory farms, run by large, multinational agribusiness conglomerates. There is not much in the middle.

In the face of this changing economic environment, Godin argues that the third century of value creation in America will not be powered by big farms and factories, or offshoring and multinationals, but by ideas. We are in the middle of the reign of the knowledge worker, and this structural change is becoming an integral part of the fabric of modern America. Godin goes on to say that "nobody has a clue how to farm for ideas."[1]

Godin wrote these words back in 2001. Lucky for him and for us, that's no longer true.

This idea of "farming for ideas" is exactly what the IGNITE Framework is all about. We are going to teach you how to farm for ideas throughout the rest of this book. First things first: Let's get organized and plant the seeds that will allow you to better cultivate your ideas down the road.

Organizational Structures

First, let's revisit what we talked about in earlier chapters. What is your organizational culture and the structure that comes out of it? Define that and you can proceed.

Traditional versus organic organizations

We have found that innovation initiatives can work in much the same

---

1 Seth Godin, *Unleashing the Ideavirus* (New York: Hyperion, 2001).

way a typical traditional organization works: through a rigid system of employees, middle management, and management. Therefore, formal innovation systems can thrive in these mechanistic organizations. The process becomes a regimented effort that meshes well with a traditional hierarchical and vertical company.

The challenge in these environments, however, is in coaxing more creative and unconventional ideas to the surface. Think of a company that has complex spans (meaning the number of people who report to one person). Or, perhaps a better way to visualize it: a company with a lot of boxes linked to a lot of other boxes, with a couple of dotted lines thrown in for good measure.

Open innovation within the IGNITE Framework can also succeed in more organic organizational structures. In areas of organizations where there is an existing free flow of ideas, an innovation initiative can give some structure and formality where there is none otherwise. People may well have great ideas that become products, programs, and policies but may have no clue what to do when those ideas spark. With a flat and well-matrixed organization, an IGNITE initiative may not generate a large volume of ideas because the organization is already actively collaborating. An innovation initiative may be ancillary and unnecessary. Many consulting firms have this type of organizational structure, as do many startups and smaller nonprofits.

Importance of organizational design

Great leadership teams know that, to be effective, they must organize their enterprise in a way that delivers the most value to their customers, employees, and shareholders. The organizational design element is critical to how ideas move through organizations and is foundational to how you build your innovation center.

Your organizational design might be traditional or organic or something in between. Regardless of whether your organization is designed around products, geographies, lines of business or key customers, the key is to understand what the organizational goals are and how the organizational design supports those goals. Understanding those two elements will enable you to position the innovation center at the heart of product and value creation.

Traditionally, organizations are classified as either predominantly sales-driven or predominantly marketing-driven. We've learned that the crux of the innovation work occurs where you may assume it would: under the vice president of marketing in marketing-focused organizations and under the vice president of sales in sales-focused organizations. Understanding where the locus of organizational power is in your organization can help make clear where the innovation center may best be positioned.

Integrating Innovation into Your Organizational Design

Before we get to the collection of ideas, you need to think about how to structure your organization's efforts. Who is in charge of the program? Where will it report in the organization chart? And how is it accounted for and measured? These are all important questions that will have to be answered before you begin your work.

Our challenge to you is to think about the broader goals of your organization, both at a strategic level (business unit by business unit) and at a larger, corporation-wide level. Your innovation efforts should directly support those larger, strategic goals. Furthermore, understanding those larger organizational goals will allow you to place the innovation effort, and its future output, into the right department or division.

Think about how your organization is structured. Is it by product line, geography, or work function? In some cases, your innovation efforts may be limited by this structure. For instance, placing innovation efforts into the hands of a geographically specific division may exclude ideators in other geographies. You may find all of the ideas only come from and benefit that area.

An example of how to gain outside perspective and not be locked into local efforts is the work Greenpeace is doing with its Mobiles x Mobilisation event.[2] Greenpeace knows that mobile technology is playing an ever-increasing role in campaigns, engagement, and activism around the world—creating countless opportunities and corresponding challenges.

The Mobiles x Mobilisation event provides a camp-like environment for mobile innovation, serving as a much-needed space for peers and practitioners at campaigning organizations around the world to connect, collaborate, and sharpen skills. It's here they close gaps in their mobile engagement strategies for social change while inviting in inspiration from the front lines of mobile innovation—via industry leaders, trendsetters, and researchers. It's a fascinating model for getting outside stakeholders and industry peers involved in innovation within the organization.

Ignoring this type of inclusion work may minimize your success if efforts are set up within a department that has a narrow scope of responsibility or power.[3] Similarly, you may find your efforts constrained to the work being done in your specific product line division. If you are aiming to build a long-term strategic tool into your organization, having it located or co-located near leadership is critical. Innovation is a strategic capability and not a tactical capability to be sourced adjacent to the factory or distribution center. We can't emphasize this enough when organizing your open innovation center based on the IGNITE Framework.

Beyond organizational structure, there is always the question of which function an innovation initiative should report into. When thinking about this question, ask yourself: what is the strategic value that the company

---

2 This and subsequent information about Mobiles x Mobilisation are from an interview between the authors and Michael Silberman of Greenpeace in 2015 and from http://www.mobilisationlab.org/mobiles-x-mobilisation, accessed December 6, 2015.
3 Richard Daft, *Organization Theory and Design* (Mason, Ohio: South-Western, 2013, 2010).

or nonprofit generates? Are you a product development company that spins off hundreds of new products a year? Are you a marketing-centric company that is able to sell differentiated products through marketing and content strategy mastery? Or are you a sales organization that has a stable product and relies on a skilled sales staff and distribution schema to be competitive? These strategic competitive advantages tell you exactly where you should set up your innovation effort.

BBC Worldwide ran an innovation and ideation program[4] that provides a fantastic example of purpose-placement. The public television broadcasting company is both a content developer (product) and broadcaster (distributor). Its leadership found it important to locate its innovation effort in the heart of product development. The center was run from the creative arm of the television network by executive Pat Younge, who was formerly the BBC's Chief Creative Officer.

Younge ran one of the largest teams of content creators in the world, with around 3,000 staff and freelancers.[5] He was responsible for the in-house TV program making teams that created some of the best known BBC hits, such as *Strictly Come Dancing, Top Gear, Antiques Roadshow, EastEnders, Dragons' Den,* and *Watchdog.* Do those names sound familiar? It's because U.S. entertainment companies recycled many programs from the BBC for the U.S. audience. Except *Strictly Come Dancing* became *Dancing with the Stars,* and *Dragon's Den* became *Shark Tank.* Engaging the entire organization in contributing to 'product development', programming in the BBC's case, was critical to getting as many ideas and submissions as possible.

According to BBC magazine *Ariel,* "There is a general naivety about the challenges that development teams face in transferring a concept into a piece of television or radio. Creating our Future, as this project is called, will address that by training people about the process—whether or not

---

4 Learn more about BBC Worldwide Labs at http://www.bbcwlabs.com/, accessed December 6, 2015.
5 "Inside the BBC: Pat Younge, Former Chief Creative Officer," *BBC's* website, accessed December 6, 2015, http://www.bbc.co.uk/corporate2/insidethebbc/managementstructure/biographies/younge_pat.

they work in a programme environment—and tapping into the collective brain of the BBC in a truly collaborative way."[6]

Our final example looks at LinkedIn's innovation efforts, run by Kevin Scott, a senior vice president for engineering and former Google employee. The fact that the innovation efforts are located in engineering speaks volumes about the strategic growth goals of LinkedIn as well as where it sees its most valuable opportunities. Similar to the BBC, LinkedIn's website combined with its service is the product being offered. "It's a little bit like a venture capital thing," Scott once told *Wired Magazine*. "When we find something we really like [internally], we want to make it successful...To have [LinkedIn founder] Reid Hoffman sit down with you one-on-one to help you make your hack successful is great."[7]

Based on the examples above, placing the innovation effort as close to product development as possible is a good starting point. The challenge is not to get the two efforts intertwined. As we've discussed, innovation is not product development. It is something lighter, faster, riskier, and more collaborative. Ideating concepts to feed into the traditional product development machinery is antithetical to the point of an innovation effort. Developing an independent effort that can act nimbly and take chances is the name of the game. Placing innovation in the correct division and adjacent to the correct supporting function will amplify the impact of the effort.

Hiring an Innovation Leader

Before we talk about how to collect ideas within your innovation system, let's talk more about who should lead this new initiative. In previous chapters, we touched on the DNA of intrapreneurs and the types of team members who can make an innovation system successful. Now let's focus on attracting the best leader. Should that leader be an internal hire or someone

---

6 See http://www.bbc.co.uk/ariel/, accessed December 6, 2015.
7 Ryan Tate, "LinkedIn Gone Wild: '20 Percent Time' to Tinker Spreads Beyond Google," *Wired*, December 6, 2012, http://www.wired.com/2012/12/llinkedin-20-percent-time/.

new to the team? Are you ready to take them on as a full-time employee or would you like to consider a more interim solution? There are few right or wrong answers here, as long as the position is supported by the foundation you set.

When the folks at Visa Inc. went in search of a leader for its idea center (the Visa Incubation Unit), they cast a net for a full-time innovation manager. An excerpt of the position description is below:

> *Visa is selectively recruiting for a Leader who will help build and lead Visa's Incubation Unit. You will have the rare opportunity to work at the vanguard of payments, mobile solutions, social media capabilities, digital commerce experiences and a wide range of emerging digital payment platforms. You will reimagine how consumers interact with their money for payments and commerce through innovative product concepts, prototypes, and pilots.*[8]

Perhaps you just need some temporary help to get innovation running in your organization. Or you'd like to have some outside thoughts brought inside. Not long ago, Greenpeace Mobilisation Lab advertised an externship/fellowship program position of this nature. The opportunity was described this way:

> *The MobLab Fellow will work with the MobLab team to design and produce programs and live events that support a global community of digital campaigners and mobilisers across 28 independent national/regional offices in over 40 countries across Europe, the Americas, Africa, Asia and the Pacific, as well as a coordinating body, Greenpeace International.*

The Fellow will also have the opportunity to work on a variety of projects, including trainings, peer learning groups, global campaign support, and piloting new tests and experiments.[9]

---

8 As posted to https://www.ivyexec.com, accessed October 23, 2015.
9 As posted to www.neworganizing.com, accessed October 9, 2015.

Sample Responsibilities and Qualifications

Once again, there are no set rules when it comes to responsibilities and qualifications for your innovation leaders. Those details are up to you. Here are some responsibilities and qualifications we've gleaned from recent innovation leader job listings. This is a short list of some of the most frequently sought-after criteria from across the industry. It's valuable to understand what other companies and organizations are looking for as they seek out innovation leaders. Here's a menagerie of examples from actual job postings.

Sample responsibilities include:

- Lead rapid prototyping and piloting of new consumer experiences.

- Integrate broad knowledge of product concepts that inform internal development.

- Collaborate with external partners including academics, entrepreneurs, VCs, etc. to structure business development relationships with external pilot partners.

- Provide development services to validate prototypes for products and services.

- Define/evolve the incubation innovation portfolio.

- Advise the corporate strategy team regarding technology injection, partnering, and investment opportunities.

- Act as a "front door" for innovators wanting to work with our company.

- Evangelize our innovation agenda internally and externally.

- Leverage the Open Innovation framework to broaden the innovation pipeline.

- Foster a culture of innovation.

Sample qualifications include:

- 15+ years track record of building and launching products.

- Deep knowledge and passion around emerging technologies and social trends.

- Ability to inspire a diverse team and drive toward a product vision.

- Start-up experience.

- High level of intellectual curiosity and are comfortable with ambiguity.

- Familiarity with product development lifecycle, extensive experience with rapid prototyping and agile development.

- Ability to roll up your sleeves and apply your diverse knowledge set to solve complex problems.

Now, armed with insight into what makes an innovative leader and where an innovation initiative should sit (organizationally speaking) to be most effective, it is time to get to work. The work of innovation is matchmaking: aligning challenges and solutions. To be most effective, it is critical to fill the top of the funnel with both. The more ideas and challenges you see, the higher the probability you have of making a match. In the next chapter, we address effective ways to attract both.

Chapter 8:
Farming Ideas

Now that you have a better understanding of where an innovation program may fit within your organization, how it should be set up, and who should run it, let's switch back, once again, to Godin's words of wisdom. How will you farm ideas? And how can it be done specifically within the IGNITE Framework?

Lucky for you, co-authors Randal and David are both quite accomplished gardeners—literally and figuratively. We're familiar with the seeding, feeding, and weeding of not only plants, but of ideas. In this section, we will cover seeding ideas. Roll up your sleeves and let's begin.

Start With Employees

As we've discussed in past chapters, some of the best ideas come from a motivated and engaged employee base. While your specific organization's nuances may challenge the wisdom of turning to employees as your first source, there's often no better audience to consider.

We know the temptation to turn first to customers for ideas and innovation. You are already listening to their feedback on your programs, products, and services through a variety of channels from social media to your call center, and you're (hopefully) acting on that feedback.

However, your employee innovation program should come first. When you sit down and really listen to your customers and analyze what your customers are saying, you will find it's usually not innovative. It's simple feedback such as web links not working, invalid coupons, or "You lost my bag, again, for the 10th time." Customer service and the unstructured data that comes from that is often not innovative thinking. Instead, you would need to set up an innovation framework for your customers, but you need to start with employees—and only employees—first.

Dell's Project Sputnik

Limiting initial ideation to current employees is not uncommon. We found that this is the same approach behind the internal innovation program at technology manufacturer Dell. As we discussed in an earlier chapter, at the beginning of 2012, Dell launched an internal incubation fund to uncover great ideas throughout the company. Dell believed an abundance of good ideas were tucked away in the heads of employees at all different levels of the company. These ideas would ultimately benefit its customers, its employees, and its bottom line if given a little protection and help to grow.

Dell named three key employees to initiate the program: Nnamdi Orakwue, Michael Coté, and Matt Baker. Essentially, the team formed an internal venture capital firm designed exclusively and specifically to review and support pitches from employees. Approved projects receive a small amount of cash to fund six months of development. At the end of the six months, a project either graduates from the incubator program (by being folded into a business unit or the team can apply for more funding) or is disbanded. This follows the model of the American Cancer Society's Futuring and Innovation Center as well as other best-in-class innovation programs.

One example of a product that came out of this employee-focused innovation program for Dell is Project Sputnik.[1] Project Sputnik's end product was the much anticipated version of Dell's Ubuntu laptop made specifically for developers (currently marketed as Dell XPS 13 Linux Developer Edition). Ubuntu is an open source Linux operating system that runs on everything from the smartphone, the tablet and the PC to the server and the cloud. According to some metrics, Ubuntu is the most popular desktop Linux distribution. At the time of Project Sputnik, several hardware providers were scrambling to offer developers such a laptop. Barton George, a director at Dell, had the original idea for the company and was one of the first employees to take advantage of the incubation program.

"The XPS13 didn't exist when this idea was first proposed to me, so once that became available, that made it a no-brainer," George explained. "We had this incubation program, plus this hardware we can put it on, so everything just fell into place."

Part of the success of Dell's Sputnik project was rooted in the way the project was developed and showcased throughout the organization. Sure, the combination of cutting-edge software and hardware is something unique. But the way that Dell leveraged the success of their initial product paved the way for future project development. George was encouraged to share his experience, which validated the entire innovation project.

"Our guiding principle from the beginning was to be very open about it along the way. We've talked about it in social media, through IdeaStorm, on a special Project Sputnik tech forum, plus the Dell TechCenter. And all

---

1 Diana Ost, "Dell's Project Sputnik: How Nurturing Employee Innovation Can Change Your Business," *Dell's Social Business Connection blog*, December 19, 2012, http://en.community.dell.com/dell-groups/sbc/b/weblog/archive/2012/12/19/dell-s-project-sputnik-how-nurturing-employee-innovation-can-change-your-business.aspx.

of that really signaled to us that it made sense to develop this as a product," said George. "We marched ahead, and…we launched it in the U.S. and Canada! It's been very well received and we're incredibly excited about it."

The idea was hatched in May and launched in December, a mere eight-month time frame. How fast does product development take in your organization?

Google's 20-percent program

Of course, we can't have a conversation about engaging employees in innovation that doesn't mention Google and its unique approach. Google is famous throughout the tech and innovation world for its "20 percent time," a program that encouraged employees to spend 20 percent of their work time developing their own ideas.

How important was the 20-percent program to the underlying success of Google? In 2005, it was responsible for 50 percent of the products Google launched.[2] Think about that. No wonder Google was so proud of the initiative that launched game-changing (and highly profitable) products such as Gmail, GoogleTalk and Adsense.[3]

More recently, a Google spokesperson told *Quartz* magazine the 20-percent program is behind Google Now and Google's Transparency Report. Andrew Kirmse, an engineer at Google, goes on to describe the genesis of Google Now, specifically:

> *"Google Now started when a few of us on the Maps team thought there was some really useful information we could show you on your phone based on where you are, and so we started working on it in our spare time, as a 20-percent project… The further we got on the project, the more compelling it became, and everyone saw the potential of it."[4]*

2 Casey Johnson, "Google's 20 percent time is 'as good as dead' because it doesn't need it anymore," *Ars Technica*, August 17, 2013, http://arstechnica.com/business/2013/08/googles-20-percent-time-is-as-good-as-dead-because-it-doesnt-need-it-anymore/.

3 Clint Boulton, "Google's 20 Percent Time Projects Pay Dividends for the Rest of Us," *eWeek*, October 13, 2008, http://www.eweek.com/news/Googles-20-Percent-Time-Projects-Pay-Dividends-for-the-Rest-of-Us/.

4 Christopher Mims, "20% time is officially alive and well, says Google," *Quartz*, August 20, 2013, http://qz.com/117164/20-time-is-officially-alive-and-well-says-google/.

There were some rumors and speculations about Google closing down the 20-percent program in late 2014. Did the program become a victim of its own success? Perhaps. In a sense, the continual output of the innovative products generated a need for continual servicing and redevelopment. Google was putting products into the market with an agile and iterative development approach. This perpetual Beta (launching products that are "good enough" or "almost there") worked well for them in 2005. But it's no longer 2005. Google's consumer base has matured, with higher expectations from their Google products.

There is an expectation that Google products should be feature-rich, intuitive, and stable:[5] hallmarks of robust product development and not test-and-learn innovative development. More research into this often-touted program from Google's Senior Vice President of People Operations Laszlo Bock reveals a deeper explanation.

"It's not technically something that gets formal management oversight—Googlers aren't forced to work on additional projects and there are no written guidelines about it," Bock writes. "Typically, employees who have an idea separate from their regular jobs will focus 5 or 10 percent of their time on it, until it starts to 'demonstrate impact.' At that point, it will take up more of their time and more volunteers will join, until it becomes a real project."[6]

Another caveat to having an open and unstructured innovation program like the 20-percent program is that no one really knows what projects are being incubated until further along in the process. It seems as if it is incumbent on engineers to find and form their own teams ad hoc. While we can only speculate, we wonder: Does this create unnecessary hurdles?

In the end, the most significant reason for the supposed end of the program, in our opinion, is that the program was highly uncurated. It

5 Casey Johnson, "Google's 20 percent time is 'as good as dead' because it doesn't need it anymore," *Ars Technica*, August 17, 2013, http://arstechnica.com/business/2013/08/googles-20-percent-time-is-as-good-as-dead-because-it-doesnt-need-it-anymore/.

6 Laszlo Bock, *Work Rules!: Insights from Inside Google That Will Transform How You Live and Lead* (New York: Twelve, 2015).

was open innovation at its finest—fast, unstructured, and supported. The outputs were interesting but many of them were interesting for the sake of being interesting and nothing else. Without a curation process that tied the outputs to the direct monetizable needs of users, Google was, to a small extent, allowing innovation for innovation's sake. Within the IGNITE Framework, we emphasize the importance of a review board to the establishment of guiding values and principles that keep innovation work focused on creating value.

Wider Audiences and More Opportunities

Other well-known companies have decided to include a wider audience beyond their employee base in their innovation development efforts. Many of the examples we highlighted in Chapter 6 marry the two efforts with great results. But what happens when employees are completely excluded and ignored?

The business rationale behind this move is an attempt to bring in fresh thinking or outside ideas and—in a number of cases—ideators outside the company are not burdened with the same cultural constraints. Regardless of how unbound and blue-sky-thinking you aspire to be in your idea gathering, internal employees will always bring a certain level of existing cultural bias with them. So, while they may submit concepts that are more grounded in the mission and capabilities of your organization, they may never be as far out and unique as an outsider's concepts could be.

Is that a good or a bad thing? Let's explore.

LIVESTRONG and the power of outside ideas

In an attempt to re-engage their base of cancer survivors, the LIVESTRONG Foundation created a crowdsourced innovation site for hacking the cancer experience. The site, called Cancer Hacks, tapped into the collective wisdom of donors, sponsors, and core consumers to present real cancer experiences and solutions to the pain points that are common within the patient and caregiver base.

The "hacks" on the LIVESTRONG site encompassed a wide variety of topics, from three tips for dealing with chemotherapy brain (forgetfulness from chemotherapy), to involving a cancer fighter's children in treatment, to doing headstands for a better night's sleep. Consider the value of going in search of ideas outside of the bounds of the organization in this case. It involves perspectives unique to cancer patients, survivors and caregivers; perspectives those working within LIVESTRONG may not necessarily have, unless they have been personally touched by cancer. While the cancer experience is unique, the analogy applies across industries. Automobile manufacturing, digital design, finance...every industry holds unique experiences, with consumers offering perspectives that are much different than any others within or outside the industry.

Cancer Hacks was launched in 2013 with clear rules for the hacks, in an attempt to give structure to the suggestions coming into the site and boundaries to help keep the content relevant and meaningful to the users. The rules were:

- No medical advice. Each person is unique, and medical professionals are the best source of information on medications and treatments.

- Think of a unique trick that helped you through the daily challenges of cancer.

- Keep it short and simple.

- Share to help others.[7]

Nice and simple and, most importantly, meaningful.

However, the folks at LIVESTRONG themselves had issues with Cancer Hacks from its inception. Sean Ramsey, the director, product

---

7 This information is from the Cancer Hacks website at www.cancerhacks.org, accessed March 2014. The site was no longer live as of October 23, 2015.

management, at LIVESTRONG very candidly listed for us the three major reasons it "has not been hugely successful," in his own words.

> *"It was a Marketing-led initiative and never had 100 percent buy-in from the programs team, on which it relied for go-to-market release and subject matter expertise. The experiment was modeled around a social-media, community site and, yet, a decision was made to moderate the content submissions. This is contrary to a user's expectations for a social community. And, lastly, and probably most importantly, the organization as a whole did not embrace an iterative model. Thus all the money and effort put into the project and all the learnings, were not leveraged to ultimately redefine and make the product better. It was simply looked at as a pass-or-fail scenario."[8]*

Your Internal Audience Strategy

If you're not yet convinced that starting with staff for ideas is, often, the best idea, consider these three reasons.

- **You know this audience best.**

  You hired them. You work with them on a daily basis. You know the value that they bring to the table, the brilliance in their thoughts, and how much more they have to give. So why wouldn't you want to have an ideation program that rewards them for their great ideas and engages them in helping the company? The IGNITE Framework rein employees in to strengthen the core of an organization and strives to leverage their best and brightest ideas. If you are running a successful company, with a great innovation culture, your employees will care about making it better more than your customers will.

- **It allows you to fail forward and fast.**

  Part of the challenge with launching your own version of the IGNITE Framework is that it will go well and potentially inundate

---

8 These comments from Sean Ramsey are from an interview with the authors on April 5, 2015.

your team with high-quality ideas to evaluate and test. You may have several dozen ideas submitted and have your vetting network in place to test and listen to great ideas but, while the framework and ideas behind it are tested and proven, there is always the chance that something can go wrong. Internal and external uncertainties are always a reality in business. Your innovation center could face technology challenges, budget cuts, political red tape, or other issues. These challenges can dramatically impact the progress of innovation development. There is a substantial benefit to working through these difficulties with your internal staff versus external volunteers or outside stakeholders. While never an easy experience, keeping the growing pains confined to internal staff will afford you an opportunity to refine the experience and stabilize the framework before welcoming outsiders to participate.

- **It's a more bite-sized challenge.**

    Creating and executing on a long-term, engaging innovation engine at your company is hard work. It involves collecting ideas from your employees, promoting the system to get those ideas, finding the right people to be involved, playing politics, and getting funding to take truly innovative ideas and make them a reality. The work can be messy at times and seem uncoordinated at first. While the theoretical elements are easy to grasp and our explanations give a clear set of directions, the learning curve is steep. Managing such an enterprise-wide initiative requires time to iron out the wrinkles. However, once you master this process with your internal IGNITE program, it's easier (albeit still not easy) to take the work you have done and face it externally.

We hope that we've sold you on why your internal audience is best for starting the program. And that you've seen how innovative companies highlight their best ideas from their employees and start to give them leverage to take the time to act on these ideas. This is what we want to see from the folks reading this book: More innovative companies and nonprofits doing this type of work.

To go back to our farming analogy, you've started to seed the fields of your employees, and hopefully ideas are growing. But maybe they are growing too slowly for your taste. How do you accelerate that? Next are some of the best practices we've seen in promoting innovation programs. And guess what: It's not your internal company newsletter.

Change Management and Leveraging Internal Communications

If your organization is above a certain size, you likely have an internal communications team that you can leverage. We give newsletters a hard time, but depending on your company culture those might work great. However, be sure to bring your internal communications people into the fold early on to make sure they understand what your innovation program is, how it works, and how employees will be able to participate before you ask them to promote it.

You may want to prompt the internal communications team to start talking about the new open innovation system on Yammer, Slack, JIVE or whatever your internal communications channels may be. Perhaps host an internal, once-a-month digital chat with your innovation champion or the person who directs the program. Be sure to start marketing this person and this new initiative far ahead of time. Follow the same change management steps you would for any new program or business unit at your company. This is a big deal. Treat it like one.

Word-of-mouth and Your Champions

By now you've learned that, at every company or nonprofit, there are folks who would be intrapreneurs if given the chance. One of your first steps should be to find the handful of folks in your organization that are wired this way and make them internal champions for your open innovation system.

Tap into your internal network or ask department managers to offer suggestions. Maybe potential champions even worked on a failed innovation system years before and are excited to see the system come back. These champions are folks like Doug Ring and Jason Shim, who we've highlighted in previous chapters. Approach them early and often about getting on your side and submitting some early ideas to "seed" the system.

These early champions will soon become your word-of-mouth superstars as they spread the news about your new innovation process throughout the organization.

Hosting an Idea Jam

Co-author David recently worked with a large services and former computer company to host an online idea session using their internal intranet software. This 48-hour session, called an idea jam, encouraged employees to think differently about the internal software they used and to recommend better ways to produce their current products or policy.

It started with four discussion threads highlighting some ways the company could do things better which was then opened to all employees on the intranet. The idea jam was hyped and messaged out by top executive leadership under the heading "Help us do things better." This executive push drove thousands of people to topic threads and they left hundreds of comments and suggestions. Pretty good for a simple discussion board, right? Imagine doing that with sophisticated idea submission software like GetSatisfaction, Brightidea, IdeaScale or JIVE.

Brian Dainton, a co-founder of Mass Relevance and now a vice president of engineering at Spredfast had this to say about the idea of "jamming" with your co-workers:

"It's a core part of our culture that stems from the earliest days at Mass Relevance, when we gathered after hours at coffee shops on Tuesday nights to build out our core technology and our business. We've kept this going as we've grown; many of us, across disciplines (dev, sales, finance, services, marketing, etc.), get together starting at 5pm on Tuesday night to work on whatever we like—exploring passion projects, testing new financial models, writing books, studying music theory, or just catching up on other work...As anyone with a family will tell you, if you don't set aside time to focus on things you're passionate about, life will naturally fill in the gaps. This is that time."[9]

Hosting an Internal Hackathon

Create a plan to gather your employees in one central spot for 24 hours to solve or create ideas around existing issues with your products, processes, or policies. This is similar to the idea jam we outlined in the step above but is done in-person, with some facilitated leadership of items to cover. Unlike the program at LIVESTRONG, the hackathon leverages your own employees to drive the discovery of creative solutions.

This idea is lifted from our friends in the coding world, who often pull off 24-48 hour hackathons to clean up code or create a new software program. Red Bull, obnoxious music, and bad sci-fi playing on the TV are optional in your version of the internal hackathon. What you are really aiming to do with these hackathons is to gather smart people in a creative space and let them ideate around your common issues.

Kristin Calhoun, executive director for the Public Media Platform, explains, "PBS and NPR Digital both carve out time within their resource-strapped organizations for 'serendipity days.' Two to three times a year, over a period of 72 hours, anyone who wants to can push back from day-to-day work and join a team that's building something new. At the end of the 72 hours, teams must demo working prototypes of their ideas. These working

---

9 These comments from Brian Dainton are from an interview with the authors in 2015.

prototypes are like canaries in a coal mine. They're early indicators of Level of Effort, powerful ideas and tricky ones.

"One of my favorite experiences with these was at PBS," she continues. "A team created 'Tinkerbell,' which gave our technology the ability to fly from one digital place to another while sprinkling helpful metadata (like pixie dust). Perfect example of a project that's hard to get executive level buy in/resources for. But totally sexy when you can demonstrate problems solved and potential. With Tinkerbell in place, our stuff became smarter."[10]

Idea Submission

Once you've started to solve the marketing and communication issues around your program and have started to generate ideas, the challenge of where to put these ideas comes into play. The outdated "idea box" in your hallway is most likely filled with bubble gum wrappers, old notes about someone parking in the wrong space, and probably a legitimate HR request or two that should have been addressed months ago. That's not what we want for a strong "idea submission" box for your open innovation program.

Instead, consider the innovation software programs that exist and choose one based on some key criteria. We've already mentioned several of these programs, first in the context of crowdsourcing, co-creation, and crowdshaping. The key to finding the one that is right for your organization is in finding one that provides:

- Rapid deployment and time-to-value with built-in tracking of key metrics. What's important to you? Number of ideas, employee engagement on voting, budget toward these ideas, or something else?

- Affordability with pricing for the number of admin users or number of ideas on the platform.

---

10 These comments from Kristin Calhoun are from an interview with the authors in 2015.

- Guidance across support, sales, marketing, and innovation from the software team (although third-party consulting is always recommended).

- Integration of key applications and systems within your organization. This could be with your CRM system or single sign-on to allow employees access.

- Mobile reach with multi-device experiences. Always think Mobile First when it comes to the next generation of your employees.

- An employee-centric design. You want something that will be easy for your employees to understand and use. Something that enables them to capture their ideas and for you to stack and rank those ideas in the background while building out the most promising ones.

Employees want transparency in the system. Did their idea get picked? Did it move over to another department to be further developed? Was it a "pass" in the system? Be sure to purchase a system that fulfills these needs as well. For some organizations that's as easy as collaborating with a Google Docs submission form, while most organizations need to take a look at something more advanced.

We spoke with Jessica Day, director of marketing at IdeaScale, one such vendor of this type of software. She pointed us to information on IdeaScale's website that explains "the most successful companies lose their market position if they fail to innovate; [in one recent decade], nearly 50 percent of the Fortune 500 lost their position on the list as they lost the ability to meaningfully keep pace with the market."

In an effort to help organizations solve that challenge, "IdeaScale provides software that adds structure to the innovation process so that organizations can constantly source new projects from a hive mind that helps them meet their goals. IdeaScale transparently sources ideas from an organization's network (customers, employees, or prospects) instead of expecting a small group of individuals to provide innovative suggestions."[11]

By now you should feel armed with an understanding of the first steps of the IGNITE Framework, how to market and target the right people, as well as a system for getting the ideas flowing. Our next chapter will outline the process of reviewing and testing while moving the organization further along the road to cultural change.

---

11 For more on IdeaScale, see https://www.innovationmanagement.se/ideascale-software/, accessed October 18, 2015.

Chapter 9:
Trial by a Jury of
Your Peers

"Innovation, at its core, is about changing the conversation."

— Barry Morris, Ph.D.

Everyone wants their business initiatives to be successful and innovation-based initiatives are no exception. It is true that you get what you measure and, on a multitude of levels, this is twice as true for innovation. The dichotomy here is that we are addressing not only the output of the IGNITE Framework, but the IGNITE Framework itself. Setting goals and managing expectations is the cornerstone of project management within the framework just as it is for other business initiatives. In this chapter, we will explain not only how to build an exceptionally effective evaluation process, but also how to provide the elusive metrics needed in order to claim innovation initiative success.

Creating, Evaluating, and Demonstrating Value

Extraordinary leaders know that success is based on an ability to meet goals that are set. Innovation success works the same way. Therefore, we see innovation goal-setting as a crucial first step to perpetuating organizational innovation.

One of the biggest challenges you will face in developing and establishing an innovation initiative is making the case that the initiative delivers true business value. We are conditioned to understand value as it equates to money/vanity metrics or another form of monetary reward. We think about measuring based on net cash flows, top-line growth, profit margins, and so on. While not a false first assumption, these initial ideas can set your organization up for failure when it comes to innovation success.

Corporate financial contribution is important and, in truth, any innovation initiative that overlooks financial contribution is ill-conceived. But there are numerous other ways to show value. A foundational exercise is to take the time to understand what elements your organization truly values. With this in mind, you'll be able to craft goals that your senior management can confidently support. When we speak here of values, we move beyond the strategic goals that the senior team delivers to the board of directors and the investors. This is even beyond the corporate mission statement. Think, instead, of the cultural values that drive your organization to success, whether they are written down somewhere or simply lived each day.

When you have tapped into the roots of what your organization truly values, you can frame up your innovation initiative in a way that will allow you to position and defend it to a host of stakeholders. You will have strong value creation statements which resonate from the top to the ground floor of the organization. You will be able to show how the investments are delivering against metrics those in the organization recognize and appreciate. While this approach may seem a foregone conclusion for many readers, the ethereal and nebulous nature of innovation adds a particular layer of complexity which makes this exercise difficult for even the most seasoned managers and leaders.

We have seen few groups of professionals genuinely excel in this kind of endeavor. Many struggle. Through conversations with our peers and interviews with innovation leaders, we've noticed a disparity. Some individuals clearly and easily understand the positioning challenge and others are completely baffled by the exercise.

Many grant writers, service-based marketers, and many nonprofit marketers are particularly adept when discussing innovation success strategies. We call out these professions in particular because the one thing they have in common is that they are often tasked with positioning and selling the value of an intangible. They are often used to defending and justifying an experience that cannot be touched, tasted, or seen.

Grant writers routinely compose against very specific criteria provided by the grantors, and so they have to be keenly adept at interpreting the unsaid values of the grantor and presenting the best possible case for funding. Service-based marketers are charged with "selling" experiences and, since each individual has a unique interpretation of the same experience, they must present the best possible case that appeals to the widest possible audience. And, finally, many nonprofit marketers may have the most difficult job of all: selling a feeling. This type of value exchange presents a uniquely abstract challenge in that marketers in these specific situations must consider consumer values and use those to create the transaction.

Coolness Versus Value

Many times we need to take a stand and delineate between what is cool and what is valuable. Megan Christenson, director of the Points of Light Civic Accelerator, told us "the biggest mistakes I see is what I call 'the cool trap.' I often hear entrepreneurs say, 'Wouldn't it be really cool if our product/service did this?' Or, 'Wouldn't it be cool if the customer could also have x,y,z?' Unless your customer has explicitly said that x,y,z feature is a problem, then they probably won't buy your product. Coolness [or novelty] is a very small market."[1]

Innovation as a practice should always deliver real, measurable value once properly implemented. A good review process avoids what Christenson calls the "cool trap."

You're Being Judged Anyway—Set the Rules Yourself

Once you embrace the fact that anyone involved in a new innovation initiative is being judged, be smart and set the rules yourself. Define early on the type of success that your initiative aims to achieve and make sure that you are measured along those lines. Laddering up your goals to your organization's greater business objectives certainly helps but, in some instances, contrarian innovation may be more valuable. Just be sure to identify that intention as a prominent part of your positioning in order to garner credit and not scorn.

In the same way that your metrics of success will tie into your organization's greater goals, expect to set guardrails by which you and your review team will make funding decisions. To reference the quote with which we opened the chapter: You will get what you measure because people will ideate into the criteria you set. Their ultimate goal is to get their innovation funded for development, so they will craft and propose it in a way that positions them for success in the funding process. The reality is that your funding guidelines may have as much impact on the collection process as they do in the evaluation and review process.

---

1 These insights from Megan Christenson are from an interview with the authors September 10, 2015.

Creating Your Idea Review Rubric

Idea review criteria is critical and crafting it is an exercise that you and your evaluation team should collaborate on with great care. Consider the reasons for using the criteria. What business purpose does using this criteria serve? What are the consequences of discounting an idea because it fails to meet the criteria? Some criteria you and your team will set up for mission reasons, some for profitability, and others for cultural continuity. Each should have a very distinct reason for being included in your review criteria and each should add value to the review process.

A classic rubric system can be used at this point. Like other academic or business rubrics you may have seen in the past, an innovation rubric can help review teams make objective decisions based on weighting.

Review Metric	(4) High Alignment	(3) Fair Alignment	(2) Neutral Alignment	(1) Poor Alignment	Line Item Score
Scale Throughout the Market	We have the capacity, facilities, and know-how to scale to fully meet the market demand	We have some of the key elements needed to scale to meet market demand with some investment	With substantial investment we could develop resources needed to scale to meet market demand	Even with investment we will not be positioned to scale and produce to meet market demand	
Supports Top Line Strategy	This idea directly aligns and drives our organization's growth strategy	This idea somewhat aligns with our organization's growth strategy	This idea does not align with nor is contrary to our organization's growth strategy	If implemented, this idea would work against our current growth strategy	
Drives Profits	This will drive profits above our Division/ Enterprise IRR	This will drive profits below our Division/ Enterprise IRR but at a level that is still profitable	This project will break even	This project will be a loss leader	
Market Segment Placement	This sits in open space, has no overlap with current offerings, and reaches priority segments	This sits in open space, has no overlap with current offerings, and reaches priority segments	There is some overlap with current offerings, possible cannibalization of existing customers	This will directly compete with our own offerings, and will not grow new customers	
				Sum of Line Items	

This is where understanding your organization's values and priorities, and incorporating them into the rubric, can drastically impact the kinds of innovations that receive funding. Once you select your evaluation criteria, consider weighting the criteria based on your previously determined cultural values, especially if you work in an organization that has a strong mission-driven culture. This will help align your team's funded output with the greater purpose of the organization.

Over the years, we have had many conversations with program and product development professionals about the "right" metrics to use when evaluating ideas. Their answers often reflect their own world and work experiences. Some have backgrounds in sales, some on product margins, and some on awareness and engagement. Your metrics and the way in which you weigh them are your own. To help you determine what might work best, here are some of the metrics that could be considered most valuable:

- Scalability
- Profitability
- Brand awareness
- Capture of adjacencies
- Efficiency gains
- Furthering of a mission
- Causing a pivot

Success is how you define it and, just as you can define what success looks like for your innovation initiative, it is well within your rights to force your innovators to define success in their business plan development.

The unfortunate reality is that programs will fail. Sometimes it will be a subtle failure like a concept that just never seems to get off the ground and sputters as it struggles to take flight. Other times it will publicly disintegrate in a catastrophic failure. Remember Pepsi Crystal, the Apple Newton, or Frito Lay WOW chips?[2] While failure is not a desirable outcome, it is a reality for which innovators must prepare. As such, it is critical to have the patience and perspective to be able to find value within failure.

The Value in Changing the Conversation

Innovation can be extremely difficult work, not only because it is time-consuming and intellectually challenging but also because, if done right, it can challenge convention and force organizations to think differently about the business they are in and the way they conduct it. Deep innovation work has the power to intrinsically change the conversation from one that induces incremental growth and development (evolutionary expansion) to one that indulges a whole new approach (revolutionary expansion).

As we provide a few examples of ideas that are truly about changing the conversation, consider how you would evaluate them against a rubric. Would your rubric pass these ideas through or would it give them a failing grade? Beyond pass and fail decisions, is your rubric capable of unpeeling the layers of each idea, assessing its ability to change the conversation, and identifying the potential outcomes if they succeed?

The end of the organization

We had an interesting conversation with a board chairman of a nonprofit social service organization which provides support, counseling, and educational services to parents and children. During a strategic planning retreat the chairman led a visioning and planning session designed to help all involved change the conversation about their organization.

He brought in a futurist who asked, "What do we need to do to put

---

2 Drake Baer and Jay Yarow, "22 Of The Most Epic Product Fails in History," *Business Insider*, July 31, 2014, http://www.businessinsider.com/biggest-product-failures-in-business-history-2014-7?op=1.

our organization out of business? Instead of improving the effectiveness of our programs and services, what can we do that will lead to our programs and services being unneeded?"

The Board was only looking at how they could incrementally improve, until they shifted their thinking and asked what would happen if they worked to strengthen the community so that it could nurture and support itself. Could the organization put itself out of business? Could they create a community environment that would reduce the need for parents and children to require the services of professionals?

The idea he posed is an example of changing the conversation and considering a challenge in a new light. Be warned though: Ideas that may emerge out of true disruptive conversations may not fit nicely into your rubric. Trust your rubric to guide your decision making, not to make your decisions for you.

Removing entire workflows

We also spoke with a former executive vice president of human resources at a global produce company about his efforts to change conversations through innovative thinking. He shared a piece of practical insight with us about his work to eliminate an entire workflow surrounding human resources employee relations issues.

He applied disruptive thinking to the way his organization approached and resolved human resource issues. He challenged the prevailing ways of handling things, and worked to prevent problems from happening, rather than reacting to them. Instead of looking at how the organization could resolve various human resource issues in a faster and more efficient way, he asked, "How do we eliminate the need for the labor relations legal department?" It was a total change in conversation and it started with a concrete and defined goal that was going to require a different approach to take shape.

His challenge led the team to think beyond how to improve service levels and to create an environment where that service would not be needed. The planning and work needed to achieve a cultural change is much different than improving a service, and so are the end results.

We bring these examples up because your rubric must be robust enough to recognize the high value outlier. If your rubric is only programmed to deliver additional cupholders in minivans, you should expect to see minivans in which every seat has access to at least two cupholders. Truly you get what you measure.

The Review Team

In Chapter 5, we took a look at two facets that are critical to consider when building an innovation team: work function and innovation personality. We are going to dive deeper into the importance of these two facets and introduce one more: organizational capital. These three factors should serve as your baseline points when reviewing potential candidates for your innovation review team. Each factor is independent of the other and, yet, they are equally important. Understanding why each holds value will help you gather a cohesive, highly effective team or taskforce.

Work function

A highly diversified review team is important in two ways. First, a diverse team brings with it a diversity of opinions and work history. Consider the success and failures a seasoned director has experienced. This individual has certainly seen processes, programs, and projects that had been promising on face value but, for one reason or another, imploded. Similarly, they are sure to have worked on dark horse projects that became invaluable to the organization. These years of service and insight will be important as you start to review proposals. A seasoned member can look past the ideas and into the execution plans even before the ideator moves into business plan development. That kind of foresight is additive to idea discussion, particularly as you find a majority of your innovation submissions will come from young and eager employees who will benefit from coaching (organizational politics, budget resources, staffing, etc.) during the business plan development phase.

Consider the variety of roles that you would need to involve if you were the founder of an outside startup. Beyond getting the business up and running, think of the questions you would have and the advice you would need. The external counsel, the outside perspective, the gut-checks and straw-man activities. Questions abound. Guidance is critical. Expertise is in short supply...unless you stack the deck in your favor. This is all true for building an innovation review team as well.

In selecting those you would want on your innovation review team, we remind you again to consider engaging not only the high performers but those who show promise and dedication. Look across your entire organization, ask national directors and regional managers about the stand-outs they would recommend. What is important is that these team members not only have a superb grasp of their individual functional areas of expertise but that they are able to see their work as part of a collective effort. Some accountants are fantastic at the mathematics and functions of their craft, but they fail to see how their work impacts the rest of the organization. We don't mean to pick on accountants, though. As you recall in Chapter 5, a great starting lineup would include representatives from legal, accounting or finance, sales/business development, strategy, marketing, IT, and operations.

Something that may be overlooked in your selection criteria is entrepreneurial experience and interest. Employees who moonlight, have run their own businesses, or who have been involved in a startup bring extraordinary value to the innovation process. Their experiences with bootstrapping and making their own way not only give them a critical point of view but also affords them a unique brand of empathy that will be important as you begin to develop and mentor funded innovators through the IGNITE Framework.

In these roles, individual skill-set specialists need to have a holistic 360-degree view. Their appreciation of how each person on the team can contribute and how their efforts together will intertwine is critical to the successful selection and support of budding innovations. The balance of skill sets is not enough. Having that balance within a group of natural collaborators should be your target.

Innovation personality

Beyond the work function, we explored in Chapter 5 the various innovation personalities that exist and talked about why each is important in its own right. Combined, they bring a variety of approaches that challenge the original work, explore the total opportunity, and help it develop through the process.

Part of being successful in implementing these personalities is knowing when to bring each into play. Timing is everything as you fast-track the innovation effort. Each of the personalities will naturally gravitate toward different steps of the review and development process. Below, however, we highlight how a few select personalities can and should engage specifically in the review process. These examples are not prescriptive because every personality adds value. As you evaluate ideas, you will learn how to best engage your team and use them to explore and evaluate the submissions.

Reverse Engineer personalities are eager to deconstruct innovation submissions that appear to have value. They relish the opportunity to deconstruct concepts to understand their fundamentals and, in some cases, they may find that fundamentals are lacking. Reverse Engineers are also often the first members of the review team to offer augmentations and changes they feel can add value. While these additions can help propel innovations forward, they need to be held in check in the initial review screens. It is ultimately the innovator that is producing the final proposal so it is the innovator's responsibility to craft and prove the concept.

Alchemists, like Reverse Engineers, quickly begin to think about what else they can do with base concepts that are submitted. How can new ideas be bolted on to drive additional value? Again, there is a time and a place for this exercise. While these expansion conversations allow the team to see the possibilities, the panacea visions cloud the fact that the concept has yet to be proven.

Robin Hoods have a very valuable role in the review process because they tend to have rich external knowledge about systems, solutions, and technologies. In review processes, it is the Robin Hood personality that is most likely to stand up and say, "I've seen something like this before," and then share a success or failure example. They may share a competing technology or an unseen caveat. It is their external orientation that brings in rich, new information when reviewing innovation submissions.

Librarians are the perfect foil characters to the Robin Hoods of the world. Whereas the Robin Hoods face externally, Librarians are internal experts. Steeped in organizational legend and lore, they know what the organization has tried and failed at in the past. They can help your team understand the "why" and "how" of past failures and can bring forth what's been learned from those experiences. These discussions are always valuable when similar ideas come into the review process. It gives the team an opportunity to examine how the new approach may fare better and be successful. Learning from past mistakes and maintaining corporate history helps innovation teams steer clear of predictable pitfalls and helps them ensure that the new ideas are not seen simply as rehashes of failed ideas of the past.

Organizational capital

Of the three components, organizational capital is potentially the most underrated and overlooked. Organizational capital is the clout that develops over years of good collaboration. It is the power that you have to move others to alignment not based solely on facts and figures, but on relationships and reason. The favors you ask of others, the favors you do for others, the support you provide across the organization, and your track record of professional successes all contribute to your organizational capital.

When the American Cancer Society launched its Futuring and Innovation Center, they tapped the late Mike Mitchell, who had been with the organization for decades, to be the founding senior vice president. They selected him not because of his tenure but because of his exceptional organizational capital. His years of collaboration in the past allowed him to ask others for support and collaboration in the present. Without these investments of good will, his initiative may never have gotten off the ground. Be sure to consider organizational capital and, more importantly, encourage those with whom you work to spend it, not just accumulate it.

The Dialogue of Review

Typically when we have stepped into an innovation review session, the conversations have varied both in tone, content, and focus. We want to provide some thoughts on how to effectively collaborate within the review conversation. Oftentimes, there is hidden value in ideas that can only be uncovered through meaningful dialogue and active conversations. For consistency's sake, we scheduled monthly review sessions and semiannual retreats in order to keep ideas flowing and strengthen relationships among team members.

Take ideas at face value

It is imperative to begin the innovation review process by taking idea submissions at face value. It's important the review team avoids imparting their own concepts and additions to the base idea. At this point, you must reach the best possible understanding of the idea as it was submitted. Respect the intention of the submitter and evaluate the concept as it was submitted. In the IGNITE Framework, it is the innovator submitting the idea that has ultimate responsibility for taking the approved idea to fruition. Compromising it at the initial stages without the innovator's input potentially compromises his or her ability to fulfill the obligation to transform the submission into a real, tangible innovation.

Focus on value, not feasibility

In review sessions, there can be a tendency to immediately look at the feasibility of a submission, to ask the question "Can it be done?" Fight that urge. Prevent the feasibility angle from creeping into the review session for as long as possible. Focus on the ultimate value the innovation submission could deliver if it gets implemented. Consider this perspective: The purpose of the IGNITE Framework is to find ideas of exceptional value, not necessarily to find projects that are feasible. It's then your job to find a way to make those brilliant ideas happen. This route isn't easy, and the net output may inevitably be smaller, but that is the point of the process. Higher quality at a lower volume.

Iterate with consent and collaboration

Iterating on other's ideas is a tricky proposition. As you've now read, certain innovation personalities gravitate to iterating on the ideas of others. Be mindful that—at the end of the review process—it is the original idea submitter that will create and then defend the business case in a funding request. With that said, consulting with the innovator and offering suggestions is requisite, but you must be careful how you position those suggestions.

At no point should you insinuate that funding or approval are contingent on incorporating the recommendations, unless they truly are. Case by case, your team may take the stand that the original idea lacks the capacity to deliver value unless it evolves. In some cases, the innovator will welcome the evolutionary steps and, in others, they may reject them and abandon the process. This is an unfortunate outcome of a stringent review process. You must be prepared to accept these situations because, in the end, the outcome is stronger, more viable projects that will be poised for investment and development.

Tools for Evaluation

Evaluation and implementation tools are an essential part of taking the step toward a formalized innovation center. These tools are critically important in the upstream steps in the process so that ideas are collected, segmented, and routed appropriately. Without the right tools in place, managing this process can get unwieldy once you achieve a certain scale. You may find that, at inception, the trickle of ideas can be managed on an Excel spreadsheet. But with great marketing, outreach, and engagement, you should soon see your innovation inbox brimming with concepts that need attention.

We more thoroughly discussed innovation management systems such as IdeaScale in Chapter 6 within the context of gathering ideas via crowdsourcing, co-creation, and crowdshaping. Most of these systems can also aid in the evaluation process in key ways: documentation, alignment, and workflow management of distributed teams. In a sense, these kinds of innovation management systems are designed to organize and streamline the steps of innovation development. There are many out there and each has strengths in different modes of innovation. Spigit, an online idea and innovation management tool, has staked its claim around leveraging the crowd for innovation development. IdeaScale has made its mark on process organization, helping innovation teams manage the collaborative workflows of multiple projects in development.

Documentation

As you begin the evaluation process, you may find yourself contemplating the process of documentation, specifically what to save and what not to save. The Librarian persona on the team will urge the cataloging of all notes for posterity and our preference is, also, to err on the side of preserving everything. Who knows when this same general concept will appear again in the future? Having a documented discussion around why the team funded or denied the concept may provide future teams with great insight.

The challenge with documentation is keeping the records in a coherent order and file in such a way that there is context to the commentary. Using a process management system is helpful in collecting and cataloging conversations. In several cases, we have talked with innovators who have said that their organizations discourage keeping extensive records of peer idea reviews for liability reasons. It is our opinion that repeating the errors of the past is the greatest liability and one that is completely avoidable (although do make your final decision with the help of your legal counsel).

Interestingly enough, documenting the ideas that you decide not to fund is more valuable than documenting the ideas that you do fund. Ideas that get funding will continue to grow until they are launched or fail in the proof-of-concept phase. When the team denies funding, it has an opportunity to make a statement about the potential value of an idea and even the potential shortcomings of the organization in its ability to leverage that idea. Self-assessment comments of this nature can be as damning as they can be transformative. Archiving them for internal reflection is important but so is using them to drive the organization forward to be more agile. The idea of learning from submissions that do not receive funding is a core component of "failing forward'" and something we will address in the coming pages.

Alignment

Of all the activities in the review process, gaining alignment is probably the most difficult. We want to make sure that you understand that we are intentionally using the term 'alignment' and not 'unanimous consensus.' Consensus is a rare thing and should not be the benchmark for funding. If you have done your job properly and compiled a diverse and bright team, consensus is an unrealistic goal. Alignment by an overwhelming majority of the team should be the goal. This alignment should be on the value that the concept could deliver if it is applied correctly. The merits of the submitter and his or her ability to take the concept through to fruition may also be a consideration point and one that must not be taken lightly.

Alignment is more than a simple up or down vote. In this dynamic exchange of ideas, alignment comes in the form of team members discussing what-if scenarios relating to the development and implementation of the concept, not necessarily the results and outcomes. Alignment is a mutual understanding that the concept will deliver the value that it purports to deliver and that, with coaching and development, a working prototype will prove that fact. Alignment comes only through exhaustive dialogue. How exhaustive? That depends on the idea and the team. Some teams perform exhaustive dialogue throughout the course of hours while others take days to hash things out.

What is most important is that the team is able to recognize when they are no longer moving forward toward greater alignment and have hit the point of final forward progress. At that moment, the overwhelming majority of your team is aligned and you can proceed to business case development.

Failing Gracefully, Failing Forward

Those in the innovation space would tend to agree that 98 out of 100 ideas never make it out of the proof of concept stage and go on to be fully developed products and programs. This drastic narrowing of the funnel has to start at the evaluation stage. We have seen close to a 90 percent failure rate in the evaluation stage alone, simply because the evaluation teams were not able to reach alignment. Whoever is functioning as the program manager must know that helping innovators fail with grace is a very important part of the role.

Failure is not synonymous with lack of value creation. In fact, the ultimate failure would be to not capture as much value as possible from the ideas that the team does not move forward in the process. Just because these ideas are not deemed to have the potential to grow into new products or lines of business, resist the urge to cast them off without first considering the best attributes they brought forth for consideration. Think about the organization as a whole and who else would benefit from learning about or being exposed to the information.

Failing forward is fundamental. It's a positive component of your corporate culture. Failing forward comes from a tolerance of failure when it is accompanied by learning and forward improvements. This cultural component is as important here as it is at the very top of the idea collection funnel. When submitters know that failure is an option and that it is looked at favorably, there is a higher likelihood that you will see more initial submissions than in a company where failure is not tolerated and employees are afraid to make submissions for fear of failure.

Depending on how many ideas your IGNITE Framework attracts, you may extract more value from the collection of failed ideas than from fully funded ones. During the review process, you are getting at the ultimate value that the ideas generate. A broad, diverse, and well-connected review panel increases the possibility that your team can share the failed idea with departments that can use or build on them. Extended value extraction is all about networking the failed idea into other areas of the business where the concepts can be deconstructed and the value captured.

The art of the handoff

Handing off an idea to another department is a true art. While, in your mind, this may seem as simple as sending an email with an attachment, it takes more to capture the highest value. Handoffs are the most successful when the core of the review team is aware and engaged with the broader organization and they are able to marry and match the pieces of the unapproved ideas with the structural gaps in the various departments they engage. Certain standalone submissions may not have been right for full implementation but they may have fractions of value or even inspiration that can spur on others if positioned and presented correctly.

An example of this not working was late in the first decade of the 2000's, when David was a funded innovator of the American Cancer Society's Future and Innovation Center. He had developed, won funding, and tested a personal cancer detection app for primary care physicians called C-Tools. It had been alpha and beta-tested all across Texas with hundreds of primary care physicians. When the time came to hand it off to our national organization, it had no true home. At that time there was no "mobile department" and certainly no "product team." Instead it was handed off to the web team and it quickly languished.

The web team was intrigued with their new product but they were both unprepared to market C-Tools and not resourced to drive technical developments. The department leadership was not incentivized to extract the value out of the tool, nor were they ever as invested in its success as David was. This experience, of watching a successful POC fail, led the team to improve how they execute handoffs.

Staying abreast of developments throughout the organization gives an IGNITE team a keen ability to make suggestions and share insights that matter to others. It is incumbent on the members of the team to be aware of the broader business needs so that they can proactively place and share ideas once those ideas have been reviewed.

Sharing recommendations and concepts can be fraught with internal politics. Well-networked and versed in working in the matrix environment, the Ambassador personality is best equipped to sell the discarded concept to potentially skeptical directors and managers across the organization. Showing value and potential impact is difficult enough without having to overcome the "not my idea" hurdle that is often prolific within the leadership of larger organizations. Once you are able to overcome that resistance and show that even the discarded concepts can positively impact the goals of the organization, you will most likely have department heads asking for your center's engagement going forward.

Keeping engagement high after failure

Failure can be disheartening. When you are managing a process that runs a 1- 2 percent full success rate, the reality is that failure is going to be the norm. Prepare yourselves for that reality and plan on ways to engage and retain the participation of the best and most promising submitters.

David Ogilvy, widely revered as a founding father of modern advertising, had a very keen position on engaging and retaining the best talent. "If you ever find a man who is better than you are—hire him," he once wrote. "If necessary, pay him more than you would pay yourself."[3]

When encountering these brilliant employees during the innovation process, make an effort to bring them into the fold. Add them to your short list of future potential members of the IGNITE team, turn them into

---

3 This quote by David Ogilvy is originally from a 1968 paper written as a guide for Ogilvy & Mather managers worldwide. It can be found, along with other great insights, in: David Ogilvy, *The Unpublished David Ogilvy* (London: Profile Books Ltd., 2012).

mentors to newly funded innovators, or find other ways to provide them access and interaction with the innovation process long after their ideas are processed through the IGNITE Framework.

Preparing to Craft a Business Plan

All great ideas take their first step toward becoming an innovation when they are mapped out into a formal business plan. If anything bears repeating, it is that innovation is a very measured and methodical process. While not necessarily rigid and formulaic, there is a cadence and system to it. Creating a formal business plan is an important part of the sequence. But what we want to do is encourage you not to create a formal business plan that goes on for pages and pages. Instead, keep it lean.

In the next chapter, we talk about the idea of a lean business plan canvas, its value, and the steps to creating one in advance of launching your proof of concept.

Chapter 10:
Business Plan Canvas
and Value Articulation

At this point in the IGNITE process, you will be actively collecting ideas from your target market of employees, volunteers, or customers. You'll have processes and software in place to collect and manage these ideas. You'll have a good internal board of advisors (your IGNITE team) who will be starting to review these ideas regularly and rate them on a variety of factors. Now the work shifts back to the intrapreneur. Once an idea is highlighted and approved by the internal review board, it's handed back to the intrapreneur to further develop and refine.

This next stage of development is best done through the creation of a business plan. But, relax. Our idea of a business plan is likely different from what you're painfully envisioning. The founder of Southwest Airlines, Herb Kelleher, famously claimed his business plan was written on the back of a napkin. It contained a triangle and three simple words: Houston, Dallas, and San Antonio. These were the first destinations for his then-startup airline: three arrows among the cities to show three, simple direct flights. And the picture reportedly made it easy to sell Southwest Airlines to investors and customers.

In fact, this idea of keeping it simple—simple enough to fit on a napkin—is a common consulting and brainstorming activity. In his book *The Back of the Napkin: Solving Problems and Selling Ideas with Pictures*, Dan Roam speaks to the fact that thinking with pictures can help anyone discover and obtain new ideas, solve problems in unexpected ways, and dramatically improve their ability to share their insights.[1] This is a great step for you and your employees when brainstorming new ideas. Can you draw what you want to happen? Can you illustrate the problem you are trying to solve? There's a fine balance between "the napkin" and the traditional 50-page business plan, which is an idea we will address later in this chapter.

When an idea in your program has been accepted by your review team, it's time to go back to the intrapreneur to prepare and vet their plan for moving this idea forward and turning it into a product, program, or service. In the past, an easy way to do this was to write a full business plan, one that highlights goals, the estimated return on investment (ROI), and how the hell you're going to accomplish it. Typical business plans contain the following sections: Executive Summary, Vision, Mission, Present Situation, Company Background, Management Summary, Products and Services, Market Environment, Advertising and Promotion, Pricing and Profitability, Distribution Options, Business References, and often various other related topics.

No big deal, right? You know all that without launching your business or running any experiments, right?

You can see how the simple charge to "just write a business plan" has kept millions of people awake at night as they try and meticulously write down every angle, path, or twist that might happen in the first months of their idea. As most entrepreneurs know, this business plan quickly gets thrown out the window anyway once the business begins operations and

---

1 For book information and more, see Dan Roam's website, accessed December 20, 2015: http://www.napkinacademy.com/.

reality hits. That's why we are fans of never writing that type of business plan to begin with (or paying someone else to write one for you).

Three Steps to Avoiding Business Plan Purgatory

There are literally hundreds of templates online for business plans when you search for the term. And there are even businesses that claim to be the "Uber of business plans"—companies that will "auto-write" a formal business plan for you based on key terms.[2] That can't possibly work, can it? Don't bother finding out. Throw that business plan out the window before you even start.

Instead, we firmly believe in three key ways for intrapreneurs to take an approved idea within the IGNITE Framework and further develop it: SWOT analysis, The Lean Canvas, and the OGST framework. These are not in any particular order but we do believe all three are necessary to really prove an idea and to get it prepped for success within your organization. The smartest intrapreneurs will do all three within our IGNITE Framework to truly prepare themselves for success.

SWOT analysis

Our first step is not done on a computer or from behind a screen. So if you are reading this on your Amazon Kindle or your iPad, finish this section and put it away (for now). Then get out a piece of paper and a pen. You remember those, right? Draw a + in the middle of the paper to divide it into four equal sections/squares. Now write the following terms, each in its own square: Strengths, Weakness, Opportunities, and Threats.

This, of course, is a SWOT analysis. And it's a great opportunity to sit down with your idea—and your future team—and outline the forces

---

2 Seth Fiegerman, "Enloop Will Write Your Business Plan For You," *Mashable*, December 28, 2012, http://mashable.com/2012/12/28/enloop/.

at work in and around your organization's ability to turn the idea into a success. It's not a complex process, and could be potentially done on the back of a napkin at the bar. It also helps teams gain alignment and unpack potentially complicated ideas in a surprisingly efficient manner.

Here is an example to help you get started:

Strengths	Weaknesses
• A strong brand	• Poor brand awareness
• Patents	• Lack of trust from customers
• Trademarks	• High costs
• Experienced team	• Low margin
• Strong marketing channels	• Physical space needed
Opportunities	**Threats**
• Niche market	• Lack of candidates for job positions
• No brand awareness	• Shift in customer behavior
• New technology	• Not understanding changing
• Regulations change	generational differences
• New political party in office	• Changing regulatory environment
• Shifting internal department	• Shifting internal department
structures	structures
• Mergers and acquisitions	• Mergers and acquisitions

Did you notice an overlap in a few areas? Some opportunities could also be threats or weaknesses and vice versa. And some are opposing forces that can be surprisingly interconnected. Take the strength of an amazing team versus the threat of shifting internal department structures as well as mergers and acquisitions, for example. Imagine an amazing idea that is approved by the IGNITE team, but then management lays off half that team. Where does your idea stand? Do you have strong executive leadership to back the idea or does it fade away? These are things that are great to have written down. It gives you the ability to create action plans to leverage the positives and work around the negatives. Just don't forget to update them every couple of months, as your team and project move forward.

The Lean Canvas

The second step in throwing the traditional business plan out the window is something called the Lean Canvas. This was developed by David's colleague and fellow Austinite Ash Maurya and based on the work of Alex Osterwalder and his book *Business Model Generation*. Maurya decided to build the Lean Canvas for the following reasons:

> *"I had found the initial Business Model Canvases I created back in August 2009 missing on things I'd consider very high risk while other things on the canvas didn't register as high enough risk. Because the canvas is already quite space constrained, it was important to maximize on the signal-to-noise ratio...Most startups fail, not because they fail to build what they set out to build, but because they waste time, money, and effort building the wrong product. I attribute a significant contributor to this failure to a lack of proper 'problem understanding' from the start."*[3]

Look at it this way: Once you understand the problem, you are then in the best position to define a possible solution. This brings us to another important point. When filling out the Lean Canvas online you might find that your thinking has shifted; that your idea has pivoted this way or another way. Or that your idea might not work at all. All of this critical thinking is great, and needs to be done. Just make sure that, if you and your team's thinking have changed, you let your review team know. And if you are the admin of the IGNITE program, check in with your team at this critical point. You may need to revisit what they uncover as they complete their Lean Canvas and how those changes affect the original plan.

---

3 See http://leanstack.com/why-lean-canvas/, accessed January 11, 2016.

That said, the Lean Canvas is an extraordinary way to get your "business plan" on to one page. David has used the Lean Canvas for several initiatives and found it helpful as he planned and launched two startups: The Weird Homes Tour and FyleStyle.[4] Much like Osterwalder's work, the Lean Canvas helps replace the traditional business plan with a cleaner framework that gets straight to the point. Here's an example from Maurya's website. This particular example is for a cloud-based, photo-sharing service for parents:

Cloudfire-Parents

PROBLEM	SOLUTION	UNIQUE VALUE PROPOSITION		UNFAIR ADVANTAGE	CUSTOMER SEGMENTS
Sharing lots of photos/videos is time consuming. Parents have no free time There is lots of external demand on this content	Instant no-upload sharing. iPhoto/folders inegration. Better Notification tools.	Get back to the more important things in your life. Faster. Share your entire photo and video library in under 5 minutes.		Community	Parents (creators) Family and friends (viewers) **EARLY ADOPTERS** Parents with young kids
EXISTING ALTERNATIVES Flickr Pro, SmugMug, Apple Mobile Me, Facebook	**KEY METRICS** Key action: sharing an album/video Success metric: Build a $5M/yr business	**HIGH-LEVEL CONCEPT** Photo and video sharing without the uploading.		**CHANNELS** Friends Daycare Birthday Parties Adwords Word of Mouth Facebook	
COST STRUCTURE Hosting costs - heroku (currently $0) People costs - 40 hours *$65/hr = $10k/mo			**REVENUE STREAMS** 30-day free trial @ $49/yr		
Lean Canvas is adapted from The Business Model Canvas BusinessModelGeneration.com and is licensed under the Creative Commons Attribution=Share Alike 3.0 Un-ported License.					

The Lean Canvas for Cloud Fire[5]

As you can see from this example, the canvas separates the ideas around a business into sections that are highly dependent on each other. As you may already know, silos don't work. So each section aligns with other sections. The sections are:

---

4 Find out more about these projects at www.weirdhomestour.com and at www.fylestyle.com.
5 This image is available at https://app.leanstack.com/images/cloudfire-canvas.png, accessed October 20, 2015.

Problem: This is your classic problem statement. What is it you are trying to solve? Think about the problem from the customer's point of view first, independent of any ideas to solve the problem. Remember the advice of noted startup founder Dave McClure, "Customers care about their problems—not your solution."

Existing Alternatives: Who else is doing what you want to do? Look inside your organization or outside at other competitors. Come back to this when you have the time to do a large competitive analysis. And keep updating it over time. The Lean Canvas, at www.leanstack.com, is hosted on a website. Your work is saved and backed up to the cloud. More importantly, it is a living document that needs and demands regular attention to be supremely effective.

Solution: How are you making your customers', volunteers', or donors' lives easier? How are you solving the issue that you identified in the problem statement? Again, approach this from your customer's point of view, not your own. In this section, Maurya recommends you not get carried away but "simply outline a possible solution for each problem." And then move on. Don't venture into tactics, which is the third and final step.

Key Metrics: How can we measure the success of this product or idea? How does what you want to measure relate back to the objectives you want to obtain? Your key metrics could be sales, or people attending your event, or penetration of market awareness. Just make sure it's something that you can measure and that it's something that matters (not vanity metrics like how many Facebook likes or Twitter followers you have).

Unique Value Proposition: What is the "wow factor" of this idea? What value does it bring to your customer? This should be written as a statement. It should be definitive and compelling. If you cannot articulate your value clearly, go back and reconsider exactly what problem you are solving and how you are solving it.

High-Level Concept: This is simple. Just tell us what the idea is. Give yourself two to three sentences at most to explain what you are trying to do. For Lights. Camera. Help., an organization David founded, the high-level concept is to "connect filmmakers to nonprofits to help nonprofits tell better stories."[6] It's direct and to the point.

Unfair Advantage: What's your angle? What is the one resource you have that your competitor does not? What's going to get you attention and make people stop and notice? What's going to get them to buy your product? Maybe it's the amazing talent you hire or a remarkable patent your organization holds. What is powering your idea past the competition?

Channels: How will you take this idea and get it to market? Social Media? Retail stores? Online sales? Will word-of-mouth be critical to your success? List any and all that may apply. You'll be narrowing the field much later on. In your plan consider the "where you are today" and "how large you need to be" for a full launch. It will impact how you approach your paid, earned, and owned media.

---

6 For more about *Lights. Camera. Help.*, visit http://www.lightscamerahelp.org/, accessed December 20, 2015.

Customer Segments: Start to think about who your customers are going to be. Even this early in the process, you should have an idea of genders, ages, and other demographics. If you already have a website for your traffic, you can glean some of this information from deploying an Analytics platform and dashboard. This uses browser and cookie information to enable you to see what your audiences look like. If you're part of a large organization, you likely have much more sophisticated analytics in place and perhaps even a team who can help you make sense of it. Once you start to understand this information, you can begin to build personas that represent who your customers for this particular idea are.

Early Adopters: Who are the people that will jump all over your product or idea the minute you start to talk about it? Are they tech-savvy folks? Are they stay-at-home dads? Gardeners? Stock traders? Who does your early-access market look like, and how can you start to attract them to prove traction?

Ready for a real-world example? HER Agenda, a startup co-author David has been mentoring, is a digital media platform working to bridge the gap between ambition and achievement for millennial women. The organization provides inspiration through the stories of real women succeeding in their industries while also highlighting the information and resources needed to achieve that success.[7] Here's a peek at a Lean Canvas they recently completed:

---

7 For more information, visit http://heragenda.com/, accessed December 11, 2015.

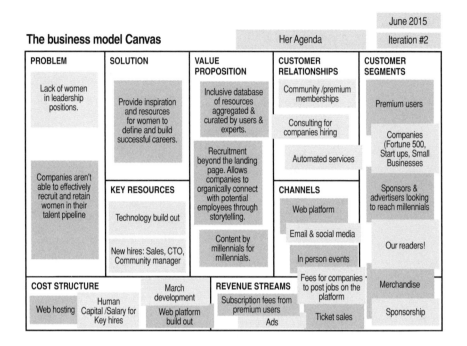

The OGST framework

Often, when consulting and running lean companies, David and Randal encourage their clients and colleagues to take a step back to really understand how the work will move forward. This is something most hard-charging, grab-life-by-the-horns folks don't like to do. If it's not moving them forward, it's not worth their time. However, time and time again, we've seen this strategic pause become a real game changer.

In the IGNITE process, this pause for strategy comes right after finishing the business canvas. You've got the building blocks of your idea, thanks to the Lean Canvas. Now it's time to fill in the details. Again, this shouldn't necessarily become a 50-page business plan, unless that's the culture within which you are operating. Instead, we want you to use your Lean Canvas to create a literal "plan on a page." One way to do this is by breaking your plan down into parts in what is usually a half-day or day-long workshop. The key deliverable is outlining the Objectives, Goals, Strategies, and Tactics. Hence the term you may already know and love: OGST.

Why use an OGST to unpack what your concept is trying to accomplish? We'll give you four good reasons.

- It clarifies gaps and opportunities in processes.

- It fosters greater collaboration throughout the team.

- It defines key measurements for success.

- It documents a "plan on a page" to utilize throughout the year(s).[8]

Most of the ingredients of the OGST can be found in the original Lean Canvas, explained previously. This next step requires you and your team to drill down into a more micro view of how the idea or product will actually work within your company or organization's structure. With the help of our colleague Ben McConnell, let's break down the parts of the OGST.

Objectives: This is your big intention. These are the major success factors which move the business-at-hand forward. Objectives solve a systemic problem or do something big, like enter a new market. They are a rallying point for leaders who manage day-to-day efforts and should be easy to remember, repeat, and spread.

Sample business objectives:
- Deliver world-class customer service.
- Be excellent at customer loyalty.
- Be an employer of choice.

---

8 For a great visual representation of this idea, visit: http://www.churchofthecustomer.com/.a/6a00d83451c5 2869e20133efa133cf970b-800wi, accessed December 20, 2015.

Goals: A goal is measured impact. It quantifies the success of your objectives. There should be at least one measurable goal for every objective. Goals determine how you fulfill an objective. Multiple goals can—and should—support a single objective. A goal to "attain a Net Promoter Score (NPS) of 59" can support multiple objectives such as "become a word-of-mouth success story" and "deliver world-class service."

Sample business goals:

- Increase positive share of voice by 15 percent by end of year.
- Build out 4 new channels in FY15Q2.
- Grow market share in a category by 10 percent.
- Hire 85 percent of preferred MBAs.

Strategies: A strategy is integrated thinking. It's your approach to achieving your goals and is multi-year in scope. A strategy reflects something that you want to get really good at as a team and you can demonstrate continuous improvement against. It describes action and begins with a verb: create, hire, develop, launch, etc. Each strategy is supported by a series of specific tactics.

Sample business strategies:

- Increase collaboration with partners.
- Identify and activate product enthusiasts.
- Enable employee engagement on social channels.

Tactics: Tactics are the process to create action in the field. They are the means to accomplish your goals. Multiple tactics are needed to achieve a single goal. Tactics should be very specific and are actions that are best when preceded by a verb. Each tactic has an owner who may rely on the work of multiple people to execute against it. And each tactic typically has its own plan, whether as a business case, a spreadsheet, or a formal proposal.

Sample business tactics:

- Develop social media playbook.
- Define social media operational team.
- Update hiring plan.
- Increase trade promotion budgets.[9]

That's a lot of information to bring forward in this process, but you really have to understand the parts of OGST if you are going to use it to implement and prove your idea to management as you move forward in your innovation work.

Another way to understand this is to take your audience through an example. An easy-to-understand example is scaling Mt. Everest (something neither of our authors has done [yet] but a good hypothetical example nonetheless). The overall objective would be to scale Mt. Everest. The goal, which should have a date and number attached to it, would be to raise $32,000 for climbing gear by August 2017. Two sample strategies would be to improve endurance and learn more about state-of-the art equipment. Two tactics that would fall under improving endurance would be to ride your bike 30 miles a week and swim 15 miles a week.

9 Ben McConnell, "*Defining Objectives, Goals, Strategies and Tactics,*" originally posted at www.churchofcustomer. com, more recently accessible at Shep21's Blog, accessed December 11, 2015, https://shep21.wordpress. com/2009/12/29/defining-objectives-goals-strategies-and-tactics/.

By using this OGST framework, you can walk into a room full of stakeholders through their overall objectives, goals, strategies and tactics and gain the approval and support you need to make your product or idea into a reality. It may sound easy, but you'll need to take this information and create what you see below. An actual plan on a page. This plan does not hold magical powers but it does become an important artifact that you can use to keep your innovators on track and executing toward the larger objectives they have outlined for themselves.

Here is an example "plan on a page." Feel free to use this as a template to guide you as you create your own version for your IGNITE program.

An example OGST

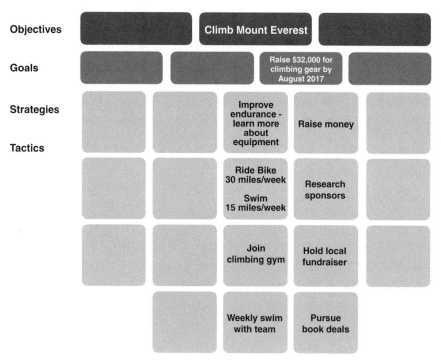

Launching Your Proof of Concept

With the business strategy and the canvas laid out and fully reviewed, your innovator is ready to move to the next step in the IGNITE Framework, launching their proof of concept (POC). As you will learn, there is a lot to be gained from launching and analyzing your prototype as a POC. The insights you glean will help the innovator and the innovation team decide if the idea is worth the full-scale investment needed to turn it into a genuine program.

Since you are working to support intrapreneurship in your organization, there are a few more items to consider and set up before you kick off your work. Unlike your friends who are in the hip incubator downtown, you are likely working within the confines of another business, which holds its own advantages and disadvantages. As you prepare to launch, it is wise to think beyond your POC to a full-scale roll out.

In the next chapter, we will talk about the things to consider and steps to take to make sure you have a successful POC trial and a smooth transition from the trial to a full-blown program.

Chapter 11:
Building and Launching a
Proof of Concept

"If the highest aim of a captain were to preserve his ship, he would keep it in port forever." —*Thomas Aquinas*

Lighthouses were first created as beacons for incoming ships and their sailors, providing a critical warning system for impending danger along the shore and guiding the ships along a safe passage. Since the first known lighthouse was built in Egypt around the third century BCE, these beacons of light have been a central tool in keeping mariners safe. Modern-day lighthouses don't much resemble their predecessors but still serve the same purpose, albeit made of concrete and steel, and equipped with helipads and state-of-the-art technology. Others that have functionally been replaced by radar and other technology still exist along coastlines, serving as cautionary reminders for passing sailors.[1]

Within the IGNITE Framework, we see the proof of concept (POC) as a lighthouse for other innovators. The exercise of developing and executing

---

1 Ian C. Clingan, "Lighthouses," *Encyclopedia Britannica*, accessed December 20, 2015, http://www.britannica.com/topic/lighthouse.

a POC is the true embodiment of the lighthouse concept, shining a light on a safe path for future projects. It exposes what works and what still needs to be changed to make the concept better.

In this respect, the lighthouse metaphor takes on profound meaning. The lighthouse that is the POC is critical because the ideas that take flight out of the IGNITE Framework are not—and should not be—inherently safe ideas. You want projects that take a risk. That's why you're reading this book. That said, the overall idea is to show others inside your organization where the "rocks" are so that those who come after you know what can and can't work; to guide your risky endeavors to a safe harbor.

This chapter covers the idea of building your POC and then evaluating it, as well as some simple, solid advice from entrepreneurs and intrapreneurs who have launched products both successfully and not so successfully. To be consistent, we strongly advocate experiencing failure and learning from it. Fail forward is a mantra that is scribbled down and taped to both of our work desks and is a key belief for every business or nonprofit we have founded.

Building Out Your Idea

The Points of Light Civic Accelerator acts as a bridge for early-stage startups to accelerate their ideas through a combination of advice and funding. It is the first national accelerator program and investment fund in the country focused on "civic ventures," for-profit and nonprofit startups that include people as part of the solution to critical social problems. The three-month, boot camp-style program convenes 10-15 teams in person and online with the goal of equipping each startup with the tools and information it needs to seek investments and scale its social innovation.[2]

This idea of for-profit companies wanting to do good in the world is profound. And this idea of an accelerator, the POCs they launch, and the

---

2 Co-author David serves as a mentor for The Points of Light Civic Accelerator, assisting the startups H.E.R. Agenda and EdgeFlip as they entered and completed the program. For more information about the organization, visit: http://www.pointsoflight.org/civic-incubator/civic-accelerator.

processes they undertake to make it happen, is exactly what we explore in this chapter. In fact, according to the site F6S.com, there are hundreds of active accelerator programs in the U.S. alone. As of December 2015, there are over 8,000 events and application submission opportunities associated with those accelerators worldwide.[3] We want you to think like an accelerator that's based inside your own company when considering launching the products, processes, or ideas that your intrapreneurs create.

Todd Connor is CEO and Founder of the Bunker Labs, a startup accelerator specifically targeting active and former military veteran entrepreneurs. We asked Connor to share with us his top six tips for launching a business.

I. **Find a customer you are trying to help first.**

"Who?" is the most important question, more than "Why," "How," or "What?" Knowing who you are trying to impact will inform everything else you do for building a product or service. Your "who," by the way, can change over time but, regardless, it is where you must start.

2. **Get out of the way.**

It's really easy to bias the results with vague questions like, "Do you like this?" or even, "Would you buy this?" It's not hard to find a way to hear what you want to hear. The more productive activity is to introduce your product to your target market and step out of the process to let them react organically. The real test is to charge people for it, which is the ultimate test of viability.

3. **Start small and hyper-focused.**

Connor hears from folks that might "size" a market at $6.5B but, he says, that's not the relevant place to start. The key question is, "Who is the first person who will pay me for this?" And then, who

---

3 For more on F6S.com, see the website, accessed December 20, 2015: https://www.f6s.com/programs.

is the second person? And the third? And so on. The way you get your first five customers is different from the way you get your 50th customer, and that is different from the way you get your 1,000th customer. You really need to have a view of this, and your business and sales strategy should look different for your 1,000th customer than it did for your first five. (Google AdWords and other paid placement, by the way, is not how you will get your first 10 customers.)

4. **Connect on a personal level.**

Really understand the person that would buy this product. This doesn't mean "men in their 40's." It means "a guy like Carl [insert picture]. He has a job, a little bit of disposable income, he lives in the suburbs but fashions himself more of an urbanite. He wishes he could lose 15 pounds..." That level of detail is critical to emotionally connecting with and talking to your customers.

5. **Listen.**

The biggest and most obvious mistake in launching a product is not first testing it with customers. You can recover from this, but the key is to be open to it. There is an expression that no business plan survives first contact with the customer, and this is true—so plan for it. "Surprise" is not an option when you put the product into the market. Design for feedback, and reaction, and input, and adaptation. It will look different, and that's OK. What is not OK is to not listen to the feedback from the market. That will sink you.

6. **Adapt.**

Your plans will change—and they should—if you listen. Connor worked with a company that launched a protein container and then heard that moms were using it for baby formula. Great, he thought! That means something really important. They are now in the baby formula business. And that's OK. When this happens, don't let your ego get in the way. Ego keeps you stuck in your original vision even when the market has told you it wants something different. When you look at yourself in the mirror in the morning, don't let your mantra be, "I'm an awesome entrepreneur!" Let it be, "I listen more than anyone else to what my customer needs, and will not stop working until they are absolutely delighted with what I am making." That will keep the right fuel in the fire for you to keep going and building something great for your customers (and your organization, too, in time).

Google Glass versus Pebble Watch

"Is there anyone in the audience tonight wearing Google Glass?" asked co-author David, while hosting the stand-up comedy show The Dilla Dirt Comedy Jam in Austin, Texas. A few in the audience raised their hands. David responded, "Let's all take a moment to turn and laugh at them." The audience chuckled. Then David added, "I kid. Really, what we just did was identify all the people who work for Google." The audience laughed at this en masse. This was a familiar sentiment repeated all over the U.S. in 2014 and into 2015, with some critics dubbing Google Glass the Ford Edsel of tech products.[4] Besides being the butt of many jokes, what happened to Google Glass? What can we learn from the lighthouse that Google built? What valuable lessons are there to glean from their public experience, and what has their lighthouse shown us in our own ventures?

According to the *New York Times*, Google Glass was officially moved out of the Google X research lab in January 2015, destined now to live or die on its own.[5] No more glass explorers on the street...for now. And no more support for those folks walking around with Google Glasses at your local

---

4 Loren Feldman, "Thursday's Briefs: 'The Edsel of Silicon Valley,'" *Forbes*, February 5, 2015, http://www.forbes.com/sites/lorenfeldman/2015/02/05/thursdays-briefs-the-edsel-of-silicon-valley/.

5 Conor Dougherty, "Google Glass to Leave 'X' Research Lab as Nest's Tony Fadell Takes Over Project," *The New York Times*, January 15, 2015, http://bits.blogs.nytimes.com/2015/01/15/google-glass-to-leave-research-lab-as-new-boss-takes-over-project/?_r=0.

comedy club or supermarket. Instead, what we see is a target-market change: a true pivot around who the Glass product team is building and supporting. We might all still walk awkwardly down the street staring at our screens but, for now, we choose to continue to be doing so on our cell phones.

Instead the Glass product team is focused on their new target market, concentrating on industry and business uses. Think of Glass in the hands, or in front of the eyes, of insurance adjusters, engineers, field biologists, or surveyors. Possibly even surgeons. According to Rachel Meltz of the *MIT Tech Review*, Glass could soon be "helping telecom workers debug equipment from afar or enabling a transcription service to help doctors save time they'd otherwise spend filling out patients' charts."[6]

Brian Ballard, CEO of a company called APX Labs, had this to say about the Google Glass pivot: "In the enterprise, Glass is solving a problem, where in the consumer world it's a luxury," he says. "In the enterprise people have been trying to solve the hands-free workforce problem for 20 years." Companies like APX Labs are using Google Glass to address that 20-year-old problem and are making some headway.[7] These companies are Glass Certified Partners authorized by Glass at Work while the original Google Glass (now called Project Aura) team works on its own pivoted products.[8]

So was Google Glass a failure after all? The Google Glass POC was designed to show that the technology, the interface, the back-end support "worked." That users (not consumers) could and would be able to use the technology as it was designed. Getting the product into the hands and on the faces of users uncovered interface challenges and social stigmas that would never have been identified in lab or machine-based trials. The light from the lighthouse revealed perils that existed: the public's concern about being recorded,[9] the stigma of wearing the tech, and the limitation that the design

---

6 Rachel Metz, "Google Glass Finds a Second Act at Work," *MIT Technology Review*, July 24, 2015, http://www.technologyreview.com/news/539606/google-glass-finds-a-second-act-at-work/.

7 For more on Glass at Work, see the website, accessed December 20, 2015: https://developers.google.com/glass/distribute/glass-at-work.

8 Nick Statt, "Google Glass team is working on a wearable that isn't glasses," *The Verge*, November 16, 2015, http://www.theverge.com/2015/11/16/9747058/google-glass-project-aura-wearable-glasses-no-screen.

9 Sebastian Anthony, "Google tries (and fails) to convince us that Glass isn't scary," Extreme Tech, March 24, 2014, http://www.extremetech.com/extreme/179040-google-tries-and-fails-to-convince-us-that-glass-isnt-scary.

put on users who chose to take their Glass into unforeseen situations.[10] What the POC revealed will be applied to future wearable projects and even to the next iteration of Glass. Some of the challenges can be engineered out of the product, and some are contextual that can be solved by how Glass is brought to market, and which markets it is brought into, in the future.

Contrasting Google Glass is wearable tech company Pebble Watch. Their wearable was one that people wanted from the start—and are still buying today as it goes head-to-head with Apple and Samsung in the smartwatch market. We talked to David Woodland, former product manager at Pebble Watch, about what they did right.

IGNITE Authors: When testing and building a product, what's the most important thing to concentrate on?

Woodland: The "most important thing" is focusing on the most important thing. Often with technology products, makers have a list of 1,000 features that would make their product more awesome. Good products and makers of them will ignore 995+ of those features and do a few things extremely well.

IGNITE Authors: When testing and building a product, what's the biggest mistake people make?

Woodland: Trying to appeal to everyone. Often with technology, tradeoffs [are made in] performance and function (i.e., higher-powered screen and short battery life versus low-powered screen and long battery life). You can rarely have your cake and eat it, too. It is essential to have a strong grasp of self-awareness and an

10 Dante D'Orazio, "Larry Page on Robert Scoble's Google Glass stunt: 'I really didn't appreciate the shower photo," *The Verge*, May 15, 2013, http://www.theverge.com/2013/5/15/4333656/larry-page-teases-robert-scoble-for-nude-google-glass-photo.

understanding of what the product is and isn't. Your product won't appeal to every person in the world, but there will be people who want the product's strengths and can look past some weaknesses.

IGNITE Authors: When launching a product, what's the key to a solid go-to-market strategy?

Woodland: Pebble has twice used crowdfunding (Kickstarter) as a launch platform. I think this is an amazing way to tell a story, validate the demand for a product, get quality feedback from real customers before the product is finalized, and mitigate a lot of the risks involved with trying to make and sell something. Crowdfunding allows the maker to have a forecast on total demand, splits between SKUs, and can help with early investment costs.

As far as launches go, I am a believer that a great product will sell itself. If it's awesome, the press often gets the word out. Marketing can speed up the sales [during] a product launch but, if the product lasts on the market, it is because it is a great product.

We also interviewed James Young, former vice president of product at Austin-based startup SparkCognition, who echoes this idea of the minimum viable product that Woodland described above, and that we described in our previous chapter on Lean Canvas.

"The absolute most important thing to focus on when testing and building an initial product is simplicity," Young told us. "Keep it simple, stupid. In other words, define a very conservative minimum viable product (MVP) and stick to that. If changes are necessary, employ a 'one in, one out' policy for features to keep the initial version as minimal as possible. After the initial version is tested and accepted—but your business isn't really established yet—gear your development efforts to the next critical feature. Focus on one feature that your users are asking for and deliver that and only that. Over time, you will build enough feature functionality to form a complete product."

Young explained, "The reason this incremental development is so important is savings. By that, I mean savings in time and money. You are saving money because you are only focusing your resources on a small set of features you know are needed, so you're not betting resources on things you think will add value. You are also building things in a logical order, so you know one thing leads into another. You are also saving time because you are so focused on just one or two things to build, that you know them incredibly deeply and are less likely to have to rework them. If you do have to rework them based on feedback from users, you have less complexity to deal with because you've kept the feature scope so small."

As with our other gracious interviewees, he was more than happy to drag skeletons out of his closet when it comes to things that failed.

"The example of savings that comes to mind is from when I launched my own company called LookOut Social," he recalled. "The software part of our company was a social media monitoring tool for families. To get this up and running, the minimum viable product was 1) parent gains access to child's social account and 2) tool collects and presents all available posts by the child or their social network (i.e. to see what the child sees when they log in to that social network). This is the MVP definition we should have had. Our actual MVP definition included things like filtering the stream of content and flagging troublesome content. We spent a lot of money and time trying to get filters and flagging working at the expense of nailing the collection of content. Our users later told us they would have been fine waiting on filters/flagging because just seeing a complete view was valuable enough to get started. We didn't nail the first part before we started the second part and it cost us in money, time, and customer satisfaction."[11]

---

11 These insights from James Young are from an interview with the authors in July 2015.

New United Motor Manufacturing Inc.

Sometimes you launch something that's not a sexy new smartwatch or tech-enabled set of glasses. Instead, it's a new way of thinking, or a new management style, or a new process. These intangibles are just as hard—or even harder—to launch than complicated physical products.

Such was the case with the General Motors and Toyota partnership in the early 1980's that created what was called the New United Motor Manufacturing Inc. (NUMMI) factory.[12] Although it was at one time the biggest corporation in the world, things weren't always great for GM (and we're not just talking about its historic $50 billion collapse and bailout in 2009). In the early 1980s, when GM had over-extended its deals with the United Auto Workers Union, a culture of fear grew within its manufacturing plants. According to those that worked there, the toxic corporate culture was built, in part, upon the tenets that management was always the devil, the worker was always lazy, and the factory manufacturing line must never be stopped.

As the situation was once described to NPR, "At the old GM plant in Fremont, California...there was one cardinal rule that everyone knew: The assembly line could never stop." One worker confessed to witnessing a man fall in the assembly line pit...and they didn't stop the line. The supervisor who oversaw the plant summed it up this way: "You saw a problem, you stopped that line: you were fired." This culture led to significant issues around car safety, worker safety, profitability, and automobile quality.

The standard operating procedure was to ignore defects as a car moved down the line and fix them at the end of the line or in a repair lot. This approach resulted in delays, defects, and massive issues no matter where the fixing had to happen. GM knew it had problems and turned to Toyota, a direct competitor, for the answers. Not surprisingly, there was no golden ticket. Instead, the solution was dozens of smaller processes that

---

12 Frank Langfitt, "The End of the Line for GM-Toyota Joint Venture," NPR, March 26, 2010, http://www.npr.org/templates/story/story.php?storyId=125229157.

Toyota had built into its factories and its culture. The cultural approach to manufacturing was the central difference and the most difficult thing to change. Reordering assembly lines or using different components is a simple undertaking, but reshaping an entire corporate culture is monumental. An example of the cultural difference between Toyota and GM was the power that line workers had to stop the assembly line, specifically with what is called the Andon cord.

The Andon cord is a nylon cord strung up all around Toyota factories and, when pulled, stops the assembly line. Culturally, Toyota employees were trained and empowered to stop the line if they saw a car with a defect. Workers and management would repair the issue on site and then look to fix the root cause of the defect upstream to make sure it never happened again. This was in direct contrast to the GM culture of never-stop-the-line. To begin to reform the culture, GM flew select workers over to Toyota's Japanese plant to learn more about the processes.

These highly unionized workers, who were starting to be afraid they might lose their jobs if GM's factory issues kept up, began to see the light.

"That impressed me," Rick Madrid, a worker at GM, said about noticing a worker pull the Andon cord. "I said, 'Gee that makes sense.' Fix it now so you don't have to go through all this stuff. That's when it dawned on me. We can do it."

When GM's top 16 plant operations managers returned to the U.S. to implement the Toyota system, however, they faced an uphill battle. Here's where we highlight a major lesson about building a lighthouse and launching an innovation: Both you and your organization have to be ready for the change. As we've mentioned throughout this book, you need to prep your culture for that change. The managers started to implement the Toyota process changes enthusiastically, but no one was listening. The rest of the organization was culturally unprepared for change.

Steve Bera, one of those 16 plant managers, noted to NPR that no one ever sat him down and asked, "'there's some secret sauce here, what is it? How can we use it to our advantage?'" In fact, as they tried the process at other plants, the resistance to change in the culture of the line workers was palpable. "The lack of receptiveness to change was so deep," said Larry Spiegel, one of the GM commandos who worked to change another GM plant. "There were too many people convinced they didn't need to change."

Without properly preparing your organization to take up the effort to support a POC, you will inevitably encounter resistance; resistance that could codify and halt your efforts for years or even decades. The lesson here from the NUMMI partnership: Change the culture before you try to change the process.

According to James Womack, co-author of *The Machine that Changed the World*, which sheds light on the GM and Toyota difference, it was too late for GM to get it right. "One of the ironies of GM was that at the moment it went bankrupt," Womack said, "it was probably a better company than it had ever been."

PUR Air Filtration

Even with a perfectly sound business plan in place for an innovation, problems can come to light in the POC phase. Sometimes these discoveries allow you to modify your project to meet the market need, and sometimes the discoveries lead you to close down the project before you make major investments.

The team at PUR Water Filtration developed an innovation line extension for their brand. It was a natural expansion of their strong brand from water filtration to air filtration. For the brand team, it didn't seem to be a far stretch of the imagination to go into an adjacent category because, after all, the company was well known for filtering water. How difficult could it be to filter air?[13]

---

13 These insights from Marvin Abrinica are from a personal interview with the authors in October 2015.

The team set up a POC, developed an initial product, secured distribution, and went to market to test their idea. To a brand as large as PUR, this was a major foray into a new category. It was a potential game changer. But it failed. The product was strong, the marketing was exceptional, and the value statement was clear. But one component of the plan was overlooked: They did not control the HVAC units that would use their PUR air filters.

Like many Procter & Gamble brands, PUR water filters are built on a lock & key consumable model (just like a Gillette razor blade needs a specific handle and the Swiffer needs a specific cleaning pad). Why? When you sell-in the system, you make money on the consumables. Since HVAC units vary in shapes and sizes, PUR was not prepared to manage the 12+ SKUs required for launch. It was too complex to manufacture and scale, did not fit their lock and key business model, and was a low-price commodity category. The manufacturing insights pointed to these challenges, but they were convinced that they could win with marketing regardless.

Cross-functional insight gathering and consideration like this are critical in the IGNITE Framework. In the prior chapters, we covered the importance of a well-diversified and respected review team. This example should remind us all that it is important to gather diverse opinions, but to also be prepared to test them in the real world via a POC, especially when strongly held beliefs are present.

More valuable lessons

There are so many other positive lessons that we learned from fellow entrepreneurs and intrapreneurs as they launched their products. As we mentioned earlier, James Young, former vice president of product at SparkCognition, was also the co-founder of a startup called LookOut Social. Despite the ominous title, the startup was focused on helping parents keep up with their kids on social media. His launch error? Not keeping up with a fast-moving audience.

"My biggest mistake [with LookOut Social] was actually fatal," Young recalled. "We were so focused on the parents that we didn't keep our eye on what the teens were doing on social media. We went to market with a product that focused on a social network the teens had all but stopped using. While our functionality was OK, it didn't matter because the teens had moved on. Our users said I can't do much with your product because my kids don't ever use that social network."[14]

For Woodland, a potential distraction at Pebble Watch was getting bogged down in partnerships, whether it was with other software companies, media companies, or even fashion brands who wanted to make new wrist straps or colors. In the end, it didn't matter.

"Partnerships can be an amazing thing—especially as a small company working with a huge, well-known brand. At the same time, they can be incredibly difficult—whether they be in software, retail, or services," Woodland cautioned. "Some companies move at different paces. Some partnerships will compromise what you originally sought out to do. Some partners are less committed than what they are communicating to you. Some will leak things you wanted to keep secret."

While this may sound scary, Woodland went on to say that partnerships can be incredibly powerful and, in the end, often are truly worth all the effort and pains it took to work with them.

"The biggest mistake related to this is not starting the conversation of partnerships early enough," he said. "There is a lot that goes into understanding what you want out of a partnership, identifying the right partner, agreeing to the right terms (and legal jargon), and a boatload of product discussions, quality reviews, and marketing messaging afterwards. Every time, it feels like there isn't enough time. There are many more places for a product to get stuck if multiple organizations are exploring a new frontier together. Start the conversation early, or do it all yourself."[15]

---

14 These additional insights from James Young were gathered during an email interview with the authors in July 2015.
15 These insights from David Woodland are from an interview with the authors in 2015.

Funding the Prototype

A large component of the IGNITE Framework is for the team to create a fund that enables the innovator to craft and trial the idea in the POC time frame. Do not put your IGNITE team in the position of having to grasp for funding after a great idea comes in. Instead, have the funding available. Innovation happens on its own schedule and, like Boy Scouts, you and your team should always be prepared.

Every organization's Profit and Loss (P/L)—or balance sheet—is different. There is no one one-size-fits-all place for innovation support funds to be added. Some organizations may code innovation as product development, some as promotional expenses, others as professional development. The coding and reservation of the dollars is less of an issue as the end-of-year fund use and renewal. In most organizations, there is a "use it or lose it" approach to budgeting. Fail to spend the money you were allocated and you will not be able to request those funds in the next fiscal year.

But, as we said, innovation happens on its own schedule. It is imperative to amend the culture to accept this fact. One year, the innovation POC budget may not be leveraged while, the next year, it may be depleted within the first two quarters. This is why it's important to have a finance member on your team: to help manage the cultural difference with your executive leadership on how the funds are used.

Determining how much you fund your innovators is a genuine challenge. POCs are supposed to be bootstrapped, bare-bones trials—not elaborate, fully-developed programs. Use what you know about your own industry and the expense of other projects as a guidepost for how much you should grant for each of the POCs.

While at the American Cancer Society, our innovation initiative granted $25,000 for each of the POCs that made it through the review process. It was a fraction of formal product development cost and, what we demanded as bare functionality that delivered insights and POC, was viable. As the innovators in this chapter explained earlier, it was a true minimal viable product (MVP).

Here's another challenge: Give an innovator a budget and they'll likely be inclined to spend it all (whether it's necessary or not). Instead, frame funding as something like "up to $XX,000" and review the spending plan before greenlighting the POC.

And, finally, there's the challenge of revenue potential. Depending on the nature of the POC, it could potentially generate revenue. That's terrific, but it may also present a genuine dilemma in terms of how incremental revenues are applied. Plan for (and avoid) that moment when the idea generates income without a way to receive it and get credit for it. Part of keeping POCs moving quickly may involve using shared services such as a shared merchant accounts (credit cards), budget numbers, and managing the accounting and allocation internally. Enlist a dedicated set of resources for your innovation POCs to leverage. Develop accounts for each of the POCs and run your trials with confidence, knowing you have legal and legitimate financial processes in place and you are following company policy.

Preparing for Launch: Getting Everyone On Board

You must prepare your organization for a POC, regardless of how small or large it is. POCs operate outside of the mainstream operating principals of your organization. They are outliers and make people uncomfortable— and that's a good thing. However, for the POC to realize its full potential, it may need collaborative effort from across the organization.

Gaining cultural buy-in

Part of the cultural process is education and executive buy-in. We have seen organizations shine a light on their innovation efforts at national sales meetings and on public calls or in annual reports. These efforts help all employees in the organization to understand the level of commitment the organization has to these efforts. Oftentimes, employees and associates that are not directly related or interacting with the innovation process are surprised to see the POC in market and have questions or concerns about it. Being transparent and visible internally early on is critical. Plus, having an organization that celebrates these innovations as they come to market is important.

Beyond securing organizational awareness and buy-in of the POC early on, we have learned that working one step ahead is a valuable tactic. With the POC in market, you gain clear perspective on the next steps (from project termination to full commercialized launch). With that view, it is never too early to begin building infrastructure and partnerships in preparation for the commercial launch. Of particular value is the development of an internal support structure.

Setting up traction/testing

Innovation is about coordination and teamwork, especially as you move out of the prototype and POC phase and into the official launch cycle. Beyond production scale and vendor sourcing, it is important the organization has made a political investment in the launch of the new innovation and that all teams are supporting it. Without the combined effort of all hands, success may not be assured.

This means getting support from all teams, as much as possible, and having data to back up any assertion this test is going to be worth the IGNITE team's time. In our research and work, we've found some of the common innovation metrics that programs track over time are:

1. Ideas generated
2. Pipeline of projects

3. Patent applications

4. Media references or press mentions

5. Stage gate specific (where projects are in the phases of IGNITE)

6. Revenue generated

7. Internal rate of return

8. Earned value analysis, Net promoter score (NPS), etc.

9. P&L impact, or other financial impact

These are not hard-and-fast metrics since every POC is unique. The team at *Innovation Leader* magazine in collaboration with the strategy firm Innosight conducted a survey of nearly 200 innovation executives on this same topic.[16] Here are the top seven metrics within that study, along with the percentage of executives using them:

1. Revenue generated by new ideas (68.5 percent)

2. Projects pipeline (67.4 percent)

3. Stage gate specific (i.e. where in the process 58.4 percent)

4. P&L impact (56.2 percent)

5. Number of ideas generated (45.5 percent)

6. Patent applications (37.6 percent)

7. Internal rate of return (33.2 percent)

The challenge here is that there is no singularly perfect metric. Each business, brand, or nonprofit has to look at their own objectives and key performance indicators to determine what works. We firmly believe that either of the two sets of metrics above are excellent starting points for any

---

16 "*Special Report on Innovation Metrics,*" *Innovation Leader*, Fall 2015, www.InnovationLeader.com/research.

organization, large or small. A mix of these would prove valuable to a wide range of stakeholders and shareholders.

Another interesting fact is that there seems to be two categories these metrics fit into: activity and impact. According to *Innovation Leader*, activity metrics show that the team has been "busy," while impact metrics show tangible results. While both are important, it is more important to use and present the right metrics to the right people at the right time to justify innovation efforts.

An additional challenge is that, while activity metrics are constantly taking place, impact metrics take time to collect and measure. Value tracking is further complicated when the fully completed projects are handed off to a business unit or project team to implement. Who owns all of that new revenue? Again, that's why we stress collecting both activity and impact metrics.

Avoiding misalignment

We interviewed a product development director who shared a story with us about misalignment that led to the demise of an innovation on the cusp of a major breakout. The new product had come from their new innovations channel and not through the traditional product development stream. The POC was put into place as a special test and outside of the normal sales organization workflows. As the tests were ending and the retailers were sending back positive data, the innovation team deemed the product line ready for a full launch.

The insurmountable hurdle was the company's sales organization, which did not have visibility and was not brought into discussion about the new line. For reasons only they know, the sales team did not aggressively sell the product to the customers. They did not take a stand and push the new product and, because of that, the product line never made it to market as a full program.

Sadly, this is a frequent occurrence. A lack of internal alignment and buy-in inevitably leads to a stakeholder not supporting a project and, eventually, it fails. Part of the culture of innovation is an excitement about the process as well as a collective commitment to support whatever comes out of that process, based on the fact that it has been vetted by team members that are committed to driving organizational success.

In short, everyone needs to be comfortable with being a little uncomfortable.

Culturally, this is what the IGNITE Framework is all about: getting an organization to be comfortable with the uncomfortable. It is about getting the entire enterprise excited and engaged and ready to support the outputs from an internal innovation engine. Whether new products flow from open innovation efforts or secretive lab programs, having an entire organization on board is a deliberate way to smooth the path to success. The collective energy that an innovation program can create will drive positive impacts beyond incremental revenue. It will engender entrepreneurial spirit and excitement about the positive direction of the company—intangible byproducts which can deliver tangible results.

Understanding the handoff

It is unlikely that your IGNITE team itself is going to launch and manage your new product, process, or project. It should eventually be handed off to a team that is positioned and resourced to deliver it to market.

As we mentioned in Chapter 9, the art of the handoff is critical to master. It can make or break the innovation before it ever encounters the strong headwinds or sharp rocks of the marketplace. In practice, we have recommended that innovation teams connect with potential 'ownership departments' and managers as the innovation moves into the POC phase so they can become acquainted with the product they may inherit. Their involvement may slightly alter the course of the POC to provide the future overseer some insights. That's a good thing, as long as the IGNITE team keeps this influence in check. The goal is to make sure that as the innovation process ends, the innovation is poised for a planned and deliberate transition that leads to commercialization.

The Operations of Innovation

Internal innovation often has some of the same trappings that new product development initiatives encounter. We discussed this with Peter Bartlett, Director of New Product Innovation at ACCO Brands and former HP Brand Manager, who shared his insights from years of launching and testing POCs. His experience in the commercialization of technology and product is hyper-relevant to the rapid prototyping and POC process.[17]

Bartlett was very quick to point out that, in the act of rapid prototyping, there are sacrifices that must be made. Success will only come with dedication to speed and a diligent focus on proving the concept. He has seen POC developments fail because of a lack of focus. The POC has to be viewed as a lemonade stand: rough, fast, and on a shoestring budget. Fight the urge and the external requests to add bells and whistles. Remind those folks that this is a prototype, not a full-scale product release. Keeping above that fray is critical to maintaining momentum and gathering necessary data.

Bartlett was forthcoming in our conversation about the age-old axiom of good/fast/cheap and his approach to it during the POC phase. In his experience, there is a penchant for fast and cheap development. These are not shelf-ready products designed to meet mass-market needs.

One example Bartlett provided was a request from a product designer to create new packaging for a recent prototype of an organizational product. Floated on Kickstarter, Bartlett effectively used the platform to manage the risk and test the market for the product as it stood in the POC stage. During this phase, the project team realized that packaging would take an

---

17 These insights from Peter Bartlett are from an interview with the authors in October 2015.

additional three months to develop, approve, print, and implement. In the POC scenario, those requests should have been immediately dismissed for the sake of keeping development speed up and momentum heading forward. The rounds of iteration on packaging did nothing to contribute to the POC; the product was the same as it was before there was new packaging on it. Full-scale roll out packaging was unnecessary to deliver the product to the Kickstarter backers. Instead, the focus should have been on delivering value to the product in a way that would allow the team to learn and gain feedback.

When it comes to managing speed and momentum, Bartlett shared another example of rapid prototype development, where the company willingly incurred higher costs to move a project along faster and with more control. During the prototype fulfillment of a multi-component product, Bartlett and his team sourced off-the-shelf components from suppliers with inventory and then executed assembly locally in a job shop. Across the board, the pieces of these kits were expensive and lacked genuine customization. But they were available, easy to attain, and fit the immediate need. The U.S.-based manufacturer may have been more expensive but it offered control, direct oversight, and immediate manufacturing feedback. It also offered speed. The job shop could have shelf-ready, assembled prototypes for retail tests in a matter of days versus the months it would take if the product were custom-manufactured and assembled overseas. The unit costs were indeed higher but they needed to move into retail on an accelerated timeline, so getting the product on shelves for sales testing was the most important success factor.

In order to fail fast, you have to move fast. In this case, the test yielded some positive learning and insights. One thing that the team learned is that POCs are designed to test traction in the real world—outside of spreadsheets and marketing hypotheticals. With substantial promotional backing and key placement on end-caps in trial stores, the product performed close to expectations. The distribution was purposefully limited to prove the concept only, mitigating risk to the retailer and the company. The customer-response data from the engagement informed a carefully considered 'go/no go' production decision.

As you might have imagined when you started reading this book, developing true innovation can happen at many stages of the organization and occur at different maturity levels. It could be a simple tweak to an existing product or an entirely new product. The keys are having the right culture to encourage this process, having a process in place and having people to own that process. And of course, you want your employees and maybe even your customer to want to do this. So how do we get them to want to participate? That's what we will take a look at next.

TYING IT ALL TOGETHER

Chapter 12: Motivation and Engagement: Making IGNITE Fun

As we hinted earlier, the IGNITE methodology works best when you have motivated, engaged, and excited employees willing to invest in the system. But the question remains: What motivates employees to participate? A major factor in writing this book is that, within the U.S. workforce, one out of every three employees is disinterested in his or her job.[1] Throughout the years, trained psychologists have conducted many scientific studies of employee motivation. We need to step back and look at this from a strategic level. Most organizations implementing an ideation strategy already lack a major component in forward-facing programs: an engaged audience.

---

1 Amy Adkins, "Majority of U.S. Employees Not Engaged Despite Gains in 2014," *Gallup* blog, January 28, 2015, http://www.gallup.com/poll/181289/majority-employees-not-engaged-despite-gains-2014.aspx.

Hard Truth on Motivation and Engagement

One would hope that employees are motivated to participate in an IGNITE program for various compelling reasons. These reasons could include improving the organization's products or processes, developing new ideas or programs, competing against peers, earning the chance to run the finished program or product, or even increasing the likelihood of a raise. That being said, we know statistics and time are against us.

A recent study from the Dale Carnegie Institute shows the number of "fully engaged" employees in most corporate workforces is 29 percent.[2] That means nearly three-quarters of employees are not fully engaged (and therefore not as productive as they could be). In the same study, The Bureau of National Affairs estimates U.S. businesses lose $11 billion annually due to employee turnover. You can bet engagement is a major factor in this statistic.

Another study from Gallup[3] smashes a popular business myth: Happy employees are engaged employees. This is not necessarily the case. Engaged employees are going to be the folks who work the hardest, stay the longest, and eventually become top performers. It takes more than catered lunches to have truly engaged employees.

"If you're engaged, you know what's expected of you at work, you feel connected to people you work with, and you want to be there," says Jim Harter, Ph.D., Gallup's chief scientist of workplace management and well-being. "You feel a part of something significant, so you're more likely to want to be part of a solution, to be part of a bigger tribe. All that has positive performance consequences for teams and organizations."[4]

---

2 "Engaging Employees: What Drives Employee Engagement and Why It Matters," *Dale Carnegie Training* white paper, accessed December 21, 2015, http://www.dalecarnegie.com/imap/white_papers/employee_engagement_white_paper/.

3 "State of the American Workforce," *Gallup* report, accessed December 21, 2015, http://www.gallup.com/strategicconsulting/163007/state-american-workplace.aspx.

4 Susan Sorenson, "Don't Pamper Employees—Engage Them," *Gallup Business Journal*, July 2, 2013, http://businessjournal.gallup.com/content/163316/don-pamper-employees-engage.aspx#1.

By shifting your mindset to embrace this type of employee engagement, your organization is more likely to encourage its workforce to intrinsically want to compete, team with others, and reach performance objectives. However, as new generations enter the workforce, the traditional employee motivation structure changes. Recent Mercer studies have shown that Millennials are some of the most disengaged workers. As of 2015, 44 percent of Millennial workers are seriously considering leaving their organizations, despite the fact that they are generally positive about many aspects of working in their current organizations.[5] For those hiring and managing teams, that's an alarming statistic.

In our research, Millennials in the workforce are most often motivated by regular feedback, personal encouragement, and personal flexibility to work on outside projects.[6] With these three items, we can dive into how gamification and our IGNITE Framework can really help engage the Millennials in your organization. A properly run gamification system can provide regular feedback when employees are completing desired activities within the system. It can also provide 24/7 personal encouragement for your employees, as they earn badges and points for completing activities. What's better than the chance to "level up" when you do great things? And, finally, when it comes to providing flexibility, the IGNITE Framework allows individual employees to step up and own their own projects.

Intrinsic Versus Extrinsic Motivation

With the changing workforce demographics, we must take a long, hard look at what would really motivate the next generation of our employees to engage, participate, and take on an integral role in the innovation process. However, all human beings—regardless of age—have one of two base-level motivations dominating their working styles. One is intrinsic motivation and the other is extrinsic motivation.[7]

---

5 "2015 Inside Employees' Minds Study," *Mercer* report, accessed December 21, 2015, http://www.mercer.com/newsroom/mercer-2015-inside-employees-minds-research.html.
6 Jenna Goureau, "7 Surprising Ways to Motivate Millennial Workers," *Forbes*, March 7, 2013, http://www.forbes.com/sites/jennagoudreau/2013/03/07/7-surprising-ways-to-motivate-millennial-workers/.
7 "Intrinsic vs. Extrinsic Motiviation," *P2P Foundation* web page, accessed December 21, 2015, http://p2pfoundation.net/Intrinsic_vs._Extrinsic_Motivation.

Intrinsic motivation is the internal desire to perform a particular task. That desire may take the form of pleasure, the development of a particular skill, or a belief that it's the morally right thing to do. Extrinsic motivation, on the other hand, relies on external factors unrelated to the task the individual is performing. Examples include money, good grades, and other rewards. For instance, in the classroom, intrinsically motivated students may perform better because they are willing and eager to learn new material. Their learning experiences are more meaningful, and they go deeper into subjects to fully understand them. On the other hand, extrinsically motivated students may need "bribes" to perform the same tasks. Extra recess anyone?

Based on these examples, we should ask, "How can we motivate students?" To help answer that question, let's remain in the classroom and recall what we all learned from Abraham Maslow and his hierarchy of needs. Based on Maslow's theory, employees must have basic human needs met before they can be motivated—particularly at the intrinsic level. According to Maslow, there are five basic levels of human needs:[8]

Physiological needs: These are the needs that are critical to our physical survival: food, water, air, shelter, clothing, and reproduction. In the workplace, most employees have these needs satisfied, allowing them to concentrate on higher-level needs. However, some do struggle to have these needs fulfilled, for themselves and for their families.

Safety needs: Once physiological needs are met, safety and security become the focus. These needs can include order, stability, routine, familiarity, control over one's life and environment, certainty, and health.

8   Saul McLeod, "Maslow's Hierarchy of Needs," Simply Psychology," updated 2014, http://www. simplypsychology.org/maslow.html; The original paper by A.H. Maslow, "A Theory of Human Motivation, first published in *Psychology Review* in 1943, is available here: http://psychcentral.com/classics/Maslow/motivation. htm.

Social needs: Love, affection, belonging, and acceptance are critical needs for employees. Not only is a sense of love and belonging important at home, but in relationships with others at work as well.

Esteem needs: Some employees have naturally high self-esteem, others rely upon others to "build them up." According to Maslow, we all need some combination of both to feel fulfilled. Therefore, he classified these needs into two subsidiary sets. These are, first, the desire for strength, achievement, adequacy, confidence in the face of the world, and independence/freedom. Second is the desire for reputation or prestige (or respect or esteem from other people), recognition, attention, importance or appreciation.

Need for self-actualization: This area is focused on finding "purpose." Have you ever experienced general discontent or restlessness in your job, even though it seems like the perfect fit? Maslow identifies this as an unfulfilled need to reach one's highest potential. He wrote in 1943, "A musician must make music, an artist must paint, a poet must write, if he is to be ultimately happy. What a man *can* be, he *must* be."

Maslow dubbed the first four needs as deficiency needs, coming from things we are lacking. These needs can be met only by external sources, by the environment, people, or things going on around us.

But self-actualization? That is a growth need. It doesn't simply manifest what is lacking in our lives, but gives us room to grow. This need is intrinsic and, as such, can be a key factor in motivating employees through the IGNITE Framework.

When our co-author David was at the American Cancer Society, his motivation to participate in the Springboard innovation program came from two main sources: a burning desire to give back to the nonprofit institution that had done so much for his career, and the rather selfish desire for the ability to control his own P/L budget. Little did he know that the experience was a classic example of motivation through self-actualization. Here's how he describes the experience:

"Although I was managing three employees in our digital strategy department at the time, my primary budget was still part of the overall communication budget. It was the idea of managing and being accountable for my own budget, outside of my department, that was the biggest motivating factor in creating Springboard. Hiring my own outside creative team, sourcing my own technology, and managing multiple web teams was a very exciting prospect at that early point in my career. In reality, all of these elements had to conform to the rules, coding frameworks, and web standards; but that was also part of the excitement. Working in a fast-paced environment creating something entirely new on a new platform was its own reward."

Creating Meaningful Engagement in Innovation

When it comes to modern ways to motivate employees, an increasingly hyped solution (in a good and bad way) is gamification. As outlined in Kevin Werbach and Dan Hunter's book, *For The Win: Gamification for Business*, organizations are increasingly turning toward the idea of gamification to motivate employees. In the book, they define gamification as the process of creating a sense of playfulness and fun around tasks.[9] These tasks could be anything from completing a report on time, handling a customer service call faster than a cube mate, or enabling security officers at the TSA to be more interested in their jobs.

---

9 Hunter Werbach, *For the Win: How Game Thinking Can Revolutionize Your Business* (Philadelphia: Wharton Digital Press, 2012).

Jane McGonigal, an industry thought leader, lists rewards outside of gameplay as the central idea of gamification, distinguishing game applications where the gameplay itself is the reward under the term "gameful design."[10] Similarly, in his book, Werbach pushes us to look beyond gamification and into true game design, which is usually broken into two camps: "doing" versus "feeling."

The "doing" camp favors game designs driven by marketing and economics. This camp puts an emphasis on the value exchange of the gamification experience. It is fundamentally based in economic principles and takes a very strict view of task and reward set-ups. The "doing" camp favors incentives, satisfying needs, game elements, inductive reasoning, status, Points-Badges-Leaderboards (PBL), rewards, and making users "do things."

The "feeling" camp favors game design as driven by cognitive psychology. This camp is driven by having experiences, fun, game thinking, deductive reasoning, meaning, puzzles, progression, and becoming, well, more awesome.

---

10 Jane McGonigal, "How To Reinvent Reality Without Gamification," *GDCVault* (video), accessed December 21, 2015, http://www.gdcvault.com/play/1014576/We-Don-t-Need-No.

Doing	Feeling
Marketing and economic trends	Cognitive psychology
Incentives	Experiences
Satisfying needs	Fun
Game elements (inductive)	Game thinking (deductive)
Status	Meaning
PBLs	Puzzles
Rewards	Progression
Making players do things!	Making players awesome!

Which do you think is the better camp? Which fits your organization better?

In this book, for simplification, we are defining gamification as the practice of motivating employees and staff in new and exciting ways through game mechanics. Specifically, using gamification to motivate employees to use the IGNITE Framework to create new ideas and innovations. When using any gamification system, it's important to understand that not all users (or "players") will respond to all types of motivation. As a simple way to implement the system with this in mind, we've decided to use the D6 method for designing a game system around the ideation process, an idea also introduced by Werbach and Hunter.[11]

D6 Method for Designing a Game System for Ideation
1. Define business objectives
2. Delineate target behaviors
3. Describe your players
4. Devise activity loops (engagement or progression)
5. Don't forget the fun
6. Deploy

---

11 Joe Sherwood, "6 Steps to Effective Gamification," *Engaging Leader* (transcript), May 17, 2013, http://www.engagingleader.com/6-steps-to-effective-gamification-transcript/.

For more about these steps, consider supplementing your reading with Werbach and Hunter's *For The Win: Gamification for Business.* Keep in mind that the purpose of gamification as applied to innovation is that it entices people to participate and then keeps them involved. So if you really get hung up on any of these steps, perhaps it's time to question the need for adding this layer of complexity.

Step number four (devise activity loops) is the step about which we're most often asked. What is meant by "activity loops?" It is the act of using gaming activities to move players to take specific action within your environment. Two types of loops are readily available: engagement loops and progression loops.

Engagement loops consist of having a player take an action (submit an idea), providing feedback to that player (points or a thank-you email), and then observing his or her behavior to determine what action comes next. Engagement loops are as valuable to the player as they are to the designer. The designer can use what is learned from engagement loops to improve the system. Driving engagement and interactivity in the innovation process is a key metric, so understanding how your feedback (thank-you letters, follow-up communications) impacts players can improve how you interact with them. Like innovation itself, gamification allows you to test and learn how effective you are in driving desired behaviors in your players.

Progression loops are like stair steps. You must conquer one before moving on to the next. Think of any action video game you have played lately. (Or, for that matter, in the past decade.) In these games, you are likely onboarding slowly by defeating enemies or solving basic tasks. Then you may progress to a "boss fight" where you must use what skills you have learned or weapons you have earned to defeat your foe. Then, you may level up and progress from there. Wash. Rinse. Repeat. The more advanced a player becomes in your system, the more you must challenge him or her.

Points, Badges, and Leaderboards

Before we get any more complex, let's introduce a classic example of PBL (remember, that stands for Points, Badges, and Leaderboards). In this system, points are a simple way to assign value to activities (much like points in any traditional video game, or the currency in the Monopoly game). Badges are graphical tokens of your accomplishments; think of ribbons in a State Fair pie contest. Or, if we turn toward social media, think of the badges from Foursquare.

These badges are almost always tied to some kind of activity-based accomplishment. An example is earning the "Gym Rat" badge for checking into a gym a certain number of times. Leaderboards are some of the oldest game mechanics. Think of the Olympics listing runners' times and then visually displaying who's currently in first, second, or third. Consider the motivation that anyone with a competitive bone in their body gets when they see that they are in second place and can "win" with just a little more effort.

When we start to break down building a gamification system around our IGNITE Framework, we hope you see the value of encouraging "players" by using one, two, or even all three of the PBL mechanisms to drive engagement and key behaviors. To fully play out this example, let's imagine how it might work in your organization with a few scenarios and examples.

Earning points

First, employees create a profile in a system (or use their existing IT-approved identities). Whenever they engage the innovation system, they collect a set number of points. Idea submission, business plan submission, peer review voting, or any other activity generates points to their profiles. These points can then be tracked and translated to real world value. Perhaps after collecting a set number of points, they receive a paid-time-off day or can leave early on Friday once a month. If their idea passes the first step of IGNITE, they earn more points.

Or, perhaps, the more points an employee has in the system, the more funding that employee's project can gain when it comes time to build the prototype or test the program. We've seen some interesting applications of this most basic gamification system in several large organizations. When companies start to move to a points system, every reward/award given to employees has meaning because they can be redeemed for things that matter to the employee.

An example is the work done by the Hallmark Business Connections incentive solutions program. Hallmark (yes, the greeting card company) created a complex online software system that enables tracking and logging of points, allowing employees to turn points into a personally meaningful reward, via an online shopping experience. It's something they call building a "Culture of Enrichment" designed to break down "the wholeness of the company into the individuals that make up that company, establishing a culture in which each one can thrive. It's cutting through the clutter of a busy day to create memorable, personal moments that show meaningful appreciation and gratitude."[12]

12 "Employee Recognition," *Hallmark Business Connections* web page, accessed December 21, 2015, http://www.hallmarkbusinessconnections.com/employee-recognition.

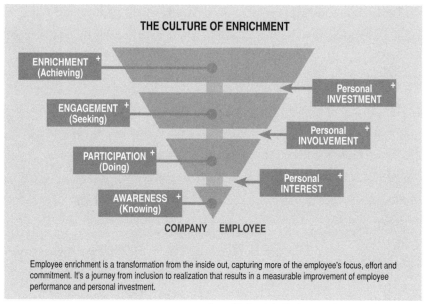

THE CULTURE OF ENRICHMENT

ENRICHMENT +
(Achieving)

Personal +
INVESTMENT

ENGAGEMENT +
(Seeking)

Personal +
INVOLVEMENT

PARTICIPATION +
(Doing)

Personal +
INTEREST

AWARENESS +
(Knowing)

COMPANY   EMPLOYEE

Employee enrichment is a transformation from the inside out, capturing more of the employee's focus, effort and commitment. It's a journey from inclusion to realization that results in a measurable improvement of employee performance and personal investment.

Source: http://www.halmarkbusinessconnections.com/employee-recognition

Earning badges

If you're not sure a points-based system will fit within your corporate culture, how about badges? Here's an example: To earn a badge, an employee would need to spark a product or service idea that surpasses "stage one" of development. We wouldn't want every person who submits an idea to get a badge. Instead, earning a badge should be a true challenge. Or publish a challenge like, "Help us improve Process X with your best idea." The winner of this monthly challenge would earn a badge. Moreover, if that monthly winning idea makes it through the IGNITE review process, receives funding, and is launched, then the innovator could gain a "Master Innovator" badge. Where do you go from there? HINT: You can graduate them and help them become mentors to other innovators, on a track to what you could call the "Master Mentor" badge.

It is always valuable to make your badges literal (at least in a digital sense) so that it can be displayed on your organization's intranet, blog, LinkedIn profile, and other places. Most often, badges translate better into real-world recognition than points do (not many outside the organization would understand if an employee listed 6,000 innovation points on his or her LinkedIn profile). According to *U.S. News and World Report,* "Many badges do more than just represent a new skill: They serve as a link, directing people to data and information on how and when the badge was earned. This was the case for Nichols, whose badge links to a page that describes the course and states when it was issued, among other pieces of information." This example is from Reginald Nichols of Reading, Massachusetts, who took an online course and was surprised to earn a virtual badge. "It was my first digital badge," says Nichols, an academic counselor at Middlesex Community College in Massachusetts, who pursued the badge for both personal fulfillment and professional knowledge. "It's something I'm definitely proud of."[13]

Making the leaderboard

While leaderboards are somewhat less useful in our system, you may be able to glean some ideas from their uses. Most often, highly competitive cultures that reward and encourage competition thrive best with leaderboards. For the rest of us, it's difficult to win employee adoption. Even some of the sales-oriented staff members we interviewed weren't fans of leaderboards. And, in the nonprofit world, can you imagine a leaderboard for fundraising folks? That's a quick path to employee turnover. Most employees simply won't find value in it.

However, if that's your internal culture, leaderboards might just be the perfect thing to motivate your employees.

---

13 "Online Courses Experiment with Digital Business Badges," *U.S. News & World Report* web page, accessed February 18, 2016, http://www.usnews.com/education/online-education/articles/2014/12/10/online-courses-experiment-with-digital-badges.

The Dark Side of Gamification

With all of its positive attributes, gamification has its dark side. Nicole Lazzaro wrote about the possible downsides of gamification in her blog post, "Cubicles are Cages for People."[14] Moving past the brilliant headline (upon which a whole book could be written), she wrote about an example in which gamification of a public transportation system could literally cause death. The example she cited is a toll road that uses a simple rewards system for getting people off the road at peak times. In her example, the toll costs $6.00 per auto from 4:00 p.m. to 7:00 p.m. Exactly at 7:00 p.m., the price decreases to $4.00 per auto. This causes drivers, on a daily basis, to wildly swerve to the side of the road, or rapidly brake, as they approach the toll booth around 6:59 p.m. By pulling over and waiting or braking (and endangering the people behind them) they are saving $2.00 on their toll payments.

Is this reward gaming mechanism helping or hurting? And if people are able to easily cheat the game like this, was it designed intelligently and is it being implemented correctly? While your implementation may not cause a life-or-death situation, it should still offer satisfying answers to those same questions. For instance, reward users with innovation points for ideas blindly and you could see a flood of sub-par ideas submitted, solely so employees could hoard points to spend on vacation days. Tie performance reviews to badges, and you could unintentionally divert attention from job-specific duties to innovation system participation. Great for your innovation goals, but maybe not so great for the rest of the business.

Balancing the Game System

The three gamification mechanisms we have explained here are examples of where you can start when developing your own PBL system. Incorporating what is native to your own existing corporate culture is a sure-fire way to get

---

14 Post is not currently live but was last accessed in 2014 at http://www.nicolelazzaro.com.

employee engagement and higher levels of participation. Why not utilize what you now know about planning a POC and do so for a game system? Try it out for three months and see where it goes.

The game company Badgeville offers a great example. Its client EMC2 has transformed its online community through game mechanics, realizing a 21 percent increase in overall user engagement. Of the community of nearly 250,000 employees, partners, and customers, document creation has risen 10 percent, creation of discussions has increased 15 percent, and video watching has increased 41 percent.[15] While it's hard to correlate these numbers to increased idea generation, it's a great case study for motivating employees to interact with each other and the larger organization.

As one of many game platforms on the market, Badgeville allows corporate entities to leverage much of the basic functionality we have talked about earlier in this chapter, allowing users to earn points and reach achievement levels. It also allows employees to carry their expertise into other applications throughout the company, including support, CRM, and learning management systems. Reputation, therefore, becomes portable, which increases employee motivation.

Within a large organization, portability may be one of the most important and overlooked features of a PBL system. Badges, achievements, and points represent a level of proficiency and help employees showcase their professional proficiency to others within social and digital platforms. These systems help employees identify and distinguish their skill sets and, in an organization with thousands of individuals, this alone can prompt success.

In smaller organizations, simple recognition from a boss or fellow employees may be all the motivation that is needed. Or the reward might just be the challenge of launching an idea in and of itself. Maybe it's the chance to do something new that's not part of a core responsibility or

---

15 "Case Study: EMC," Badgeville web page, accessed December 21, 2015, https://badgeville.com/emc/.

the chance to take accountability for an entire budget. In his book *Flourish*, Martin Seligman writes about happiness and well-being.[16] He describes a framework he uses called PERMA, which stands for:

- Positive emotions

- Engagement

- Relationship building

- Meaning

- Achievement

Seligman's theory is if an employee can touch each part of PERMA in an activity, he or she will experience the "perfect storm" of motivation. This motivation can then be turned into action at a tactical level. That's really at the heart of gamification. It is not having fun for the sake of having fun; rather, it is a unique way to position interactivity to make it interesting, compelling, and effective at driving key goals.

When you build out IGNITE in your business or organization, how will you include gamification to solve for PERMA to motivate people to participate?

Even if you are starting out at level one (to borrow from video games), IGNITE combined with gamification can give employees positive emotions about where they work. The system can let employees know that their ideas are being heard. It can build engagement by getting team members to compete for funding. It can create new relationships by having individuals work with cross-functional teams to get ideas approved and built. And, of course, it can give employees a sense of meaning by creating an opportunity to launch new projects. This last experience delivers a strong sense of achievement, when ideas come to life and turn into the innovations we want to see out of a corporate IGNITE Framework.

---

16 Martin Seligman, *Flourish: A Visionary New Understanding of Happiness and Well-being* (New York: Free Press, 2011).

Chapter 13: Final Thoughts

Now that we've reached the end of this innovation guidebook, we hope that the idea of taking the ship out of the harbor is less intimidating and that you're now confident enough to navigate around and through any challenges you may come upon.

Squash the Moonshot Mentality

We spent much of our time writing this book on airplanes as we traveled for work, and that got us thinking about the small incremental innovations we all encounter during air travel. These innovations started small, just a thought in someone's head. Thoughts like: What if our customers could listen to music in-flight? What if they could have plugs to recharge their gadgets? What if they could have entertainment in the headrest in front of them? What if we added Wi-Fi? What if our pilots came out and introduced themselves in person before taking off? None of these ideas alone are revolutionary (just as an extra cup holder is not) but, created within an environment of innovation meant to serve the needs of customers, they have created incremental value that has once again improved the air travel experience.

As innovators ourselves, we aim to push our readers, clients, audiences, and co-workers to dream big when it comes to innovation. For many organizations, dreaming big is lambasted as "greenfield opportunities" or "thinking outside of the box." Some may call this type of thinking "moonshots," in reference to former President John F. Kennedy's famous push for the U.S. to land on the moon within a compacted timeline. In fact, in the parody television series "Silicon Valley" on HBO, one character is promoted to head up a "moonshot lab" called HooliXYZ and quickly blows his budget on building potato guns and Google Glass for every employee; a perfect example of innovation for innovation's sake.[1]

Don't be sidetracked by this way of thinking.

Many executives we talk to, or read about, fear the same thing: That, as their innovation program matures, they'll be under pressure to deliver the proverbial "moonshot breakthrough." But remember, as we outlined in our first chapters, there's a thin but important line between what innovation is and is not. More important, not all innovations have to be moonshots. Just getting Wi-Fi onboard a flight is a pretty damn special incremental step.

Prepare to Pivot

It's also important to remember that pivoting is not something to be worried or stressed about. Most ideas naturally change over time. In fact, as ideas mature, you should look for various levels of value in a single idea.

To help illustrate this point, we sat down with Steve Caldwell, who is the CEO of Strap. Strap is a human data intelligence platform that uses wearable device data to market to those who participate. It gathers data from registered users' Fitbits, Apple Watches, Android devices, and more to help companies tailor advertising to the users. Just finished a run? Expect a discount on a sports drink from your local convenience store, or possibly a coupon for a massage for your sore calves, thanks to Strap.

---

1 Check out the *HBO* series "Silicon Valley" parody website at http://www.hooli.xyz/#inspiration, accessed December 31, 2015.

However, Strap was not always a marketing application. Some organizations can point to a specific moment when they made their pivot and, for Strap, that moment was February 15, 2015.

Before that date, Strap was a platform that enabled developers to build applications for autonomous wearable devices. The team had a mission and vision to empower developers to create applications for wearable tech like those made by Pebble and Samsung—devices that were autonomous and did not need a phone for computing. After a year, Strap made the pivot from developer platform to marketing intelligence software.

Steve and his team deserve a lot of credit for making this move. They made a habit of scanning their environment and being aware of their mission, goals, and the realities of the space in which they were playing. Here is what they were looking at and how it impacted their decision to pivot, according to Caldwell.

- **Technology Trend:** The team saw a distinct new reality with the launch of the Apple Watch. Wearable devices were no longer going to be autonomous, at least not in the short run. Devices that rely on connectivity to a phone were becoming the dominant trend.

- **Analytics Platforms:** Analytics platforms were migrating from the device to the phone. Developers were more accustomed to making applications that run on phones than on watches (which was where they were spending their time).

- **Profit:** Strap is a startup. Creating a revenue stream is critical. Developers did not have the deep pockets nor the interest in paying for the software developer kit (SDK) that Strap was focused on providing. Marketers, on the other hand, were eager to pay for personalized human data and opportunities to message consumers.

So, on February 15, 2015, Steve and his team made their pivot. They made the move in order to preserve the company, to insure that their investors would see an ROI, and to maximize the company's potential value.

The challenge that we all face as we are looking at innovation proposals is to ask ourselves the question, "What are all of the ways that we can create value from this idea?" When you take the time to fully explore the various applications and angles the idea may generate, you are in a position to truly maximize value. A solid intrapreneur looks at multiple ways to use and find value in their ideas.

Tips for Getting Started

In this book, we've presented various examples of ideation programs, concentrating on our own roadmap called the IGNITE Framework. In these final pages, we offer reminders and recommendations tailored to your organization's size to help you understand how to put the IGNITE Framework into action in your organization.

The small organization: 5-100 employees

- **The process of gathering employee input can be quite simple.** It could be a suggestion box (as long as that suggestion box doesn't get dusty) in the hallway or a Wufoo, FormStack, or Google form on the web. Just be sure to set the correct parameters on what should be submitted and communicate the value of the program to your employees early and often.

- **Cut the right corners.** Don't worry about the community voting process at this size. It would have such low numbers, it might only serve as a distraction. Plus, you don't need 15 people on your peer review/judging committee. However, at least three people and at least one person from your executive leadership team would be best.

Choose peers of the people likely to submit ideas as well as people who can give the OK to move ideas ahead. Rotate out the people in this group annually, and be transparent across the organization on who is in the group, looking at ideas. Follow up with every single idea to let the owner of the idea know where it is in the process, even if it's not selected to move forward. You'd be surprised how often innovation teams forget this step.

- **Guidance is critical.** Once an idea is given the green light by the review team, be sure to follow up in person. At this point, ask the ideator to flesh out the idea in more detail. A simple SWOT and Lean Canvas (as outlined in Chapter 10) could get the ideator started in the right direction. Provide a timeframe to complete this stage of the process and be sure to review the business plan with the ideator and other key decision makers in person.

- **Don't become overwhelmed by the budget.** The budget to develop the idea depends on several factors, including which of the three Ps the idea fits into (product, program, or process). Within a small organization, the budget could be $10,000 to build a prototype, to see if the idea has legs. This funding level really depends on your organization's budget, available funds, and size of the idea.

- **Set metrics.** Even the smallest organization can set up goals attached to numbers and KPIs (key performance indicators) to measure success. This is a must. As our friends Beth Kanter and Katie Paine say in their book *Measuring the Networked Nonprofit*, "If you can't measure it, it's bullshit."[2]

- **Blast off.** It's time to launch your product. Even at the smallest of organizations, this involves funding. If you have tested a project for six months, and it's working, what will you do to work it into your existing offerings? How will you reward the employee who thought

---

2 Beth Kantor and Katie Paine, *Measuring the Networked Nonprofit* (San Francisco: Jossey-Bass, 2012).

of the idea? How will you recognize them to encourage others to submit their ideas? This is the most exciting step and it's not as complicated as it sounds. When you have an idea that works and employees who are interested in its success, think about how can you combine the two to drive the best possible results.

The medium organization: 500-3,000 employees

- **Use a simple yet formal system of gathering employee input.** At this size, skip the suggestion box in the hallway. You likely have too many employees who work at different locations or remotely for it to be effective. A Wufoo or Google form on the web could work, but you should probably work with your IT department to get an idea submission form created on your intranet. Once again, you need a formal system to publicize the program and drive submissions. You also must set the correct parameters for what should be submitted. At this size, it's best to proactively challenge your community, perhaps with some of the suggestions we make in Chapter 12 or, more simply, with something we call the COTM (Challenge of the Month). Post a challenge that an internal team needs help with to the larger community and challenge your employees to submit ideas to solve it. This can be done through email, a simple community forum online or through an in-person idea jam. Once again, it's important to have transparency on how the ideas are graded and to fulfill whatever promise you made to your employees on how often ideas will be reviewed (for a COTM, that would be monthly).

- **Experiment with community voting.** At this size, it's achievable to reach the magic number of people participating to make voting a significant part of the evaluation process. But, again, you don't need to employ 15 people on your peer review/judging committee. Assign at least five people and at least one person from your executive leadership team to be actively involved in the review process. Aim to have a balanced team using the innovation personalities from Chapter 5. Rotate out the people in this group every 12-18 months. Be transparent with the rest of the organization about who makes up the team as well as when and how they will look at ideas. Follow up with every single idea to let the ideator know where it is in the process.

- **Guidance is critical.** Once an idea is given the green light by the review team, be sure to follow up in person. At this point, ask the ideator to flesh out the idea in more detail. A SWOT, Lean Canvas and other business plan canvassing tools we outlined in Chapter 10 are critical at this point. On top of that, the review team should challenge the ideator to give some thought to budget, key personnel, departmental impact, measurement, and technology issues, even if it's just an estimate and a paragraph on each of those topics. You'll also need to give ideators a time frame to complete this. Review the finished plan with them and other key decision makers in person to gain alignment. And give thought to what might need to change during the POC stage.

- **Take funding seriously.** The budget to develop each idea depends on several factors, including which of the three Ps the idea fits into (product, program, or process). For medium-sized organizations, that could be $10,000 to $25,000 to develop and launch a POC. The budget depends on the complexity of the POC. It should always be limited to encourage the innovator to bootstrap and stay focused. When David was at the American Cancer Society, he chose to use this funding to hire the programmer who worked on the mobile application. Another portion went toward building the website necessary for customers to download it (this was before app stores). The rest was used to promote the mobile tool in order to drive the KPIs and prove value.

- **Set metrics.** This stage is basically the same across all sizes of organizations. Does the idea work? How are we developing it? Who are we hiring to build it? Are we developing it in-house? If it's a new program, who are we working with to prototype it? And how do we measure it? Test, Test, Test. As we discussed earlier in the book, set up a three- or six-month POC. When it comes to measurement, we expect you to be a little more advanced in your practices than a small business would be. There's no excuse for medium-sized businesses to not set up KPIs (key performance indicators) to measure success. When David was at the American Cancer Society, he used this period to define metrics around physicians and nurses reached in Texas. He designed survey questions to ask about errors in the tool and their level of satisfaction with his customer service website. He also used it to beta test the product with hundreds of doctors and nurses. He collected errors and bugs, got them fixed, and released a new version to test.

- **Blast off.** It's time to launch your product. Once the POC has demonstrated that it works, it's time to ask how it will work with your existing offerings. How will you reward the employee who thought of the idea? How will you recognize the ideator to encourage others to submit their ideas? When you have an idea that works and employees who are interested in its success, think about how can you combine the two to drive the best possible results. At your organization's size, you can go an extra step with your internal inventors. Recruit them into becoming mentors for other idea submitters. Give them rotating seats on your innovation judging team. Think deeply about how you can use these employees to mentor other internal inventors and turn them into advocates for your innovation system.

The large enterprise organization

If you work at a Fortune 1000 business with more than 10,000 employees, here is how we see the IGNITE Framework working for you. Simply read through the previous steps we listed for small and medium organizations and then address these final recommendations below.

- **Budget for and purchase a software package to help you accomplish your goals.** Choose one that supports single sign-on for your employees, voting on ideas, metrics on ideas submitted, and a way for users to interact with each other. It should be something that's easy to get up and running. Review Chapter 6 for our thoughts on software options.

- **Budget and plan for a dedicated department around innovation.** It doesn't have to be big and complicated but, at this scale, you need employees to run this process, select good ideas, and escort the ideas and the people behind them through the complicated roadblocks that exist in a large enterprise company.

- **Make a significant investment around funding innovation.** Don't budget only for the software and staff, but for the funding that new ideas could earn. At this level, consider all the talented people you have working at your company. When employees know that their ideas are being heard, considered, and funded at high levels when they are successful, it makes people happier at their jobs.

- **Consider gamification.** Find a system that has this built in or think of an exciting way to make your ideation system more fun. For more on this, review Chapter 12.

- **Bake innovation and ideation into your culture.** Give your employees innovation time each week as part of their schedule. Help them find the time and give them the support that they need to develop their ideas into innovations. Look into programs like Google's 20-percent program that give employees a defined amount of time and resources for working on their own ideas. From the interview process onward, promote how you inspire your employees to contribute new ideas and collaborate with them to make them a reality.

Innovation is about implementation and action. Applying this approach internally should be part of your business growth strategy. It should be treated as a mission-critical component to your business's future success. We have high expectations and a strong belief that the IGNITE Framework is the catalyst that will allow you to set your organization's culture on fire and drive innovation.

It's time to IGNITE that fire.

Index